W O R D S

WRITING

O

READING

D

SPELLING

STUDENT BOOK **1**

Louise Skinner

Dianne Tucker - LaPlount

REGENTS/PRENTICE HALL, Englewood Cliffs, NJ 07632

Acquisitions editor: *Mark Moscowitz*
Electronic production/interior design: *Louise B. Capuano*
Cover design: *Marianne Frasco*
Pre-press buyer/scheduler: *Ray Keating*
Manufacturing buyer: *Lori Bulwin*

AUG 4 1993

Printed in the United States of America

10   9   8   7   6   5   4   3   2   1

ISBN 0-13-952466-5

Prentice-Hall International (UK) Limited, *London*
Prentice-Hall of Australia Pty. Limited, *Sydney*
Prentice-Hall Canada Inc., *Toronto*
Prentice-Hall Hispanoamericana, S. A., *Mexico*
Prentice-Hall of India Private Limited, *New Delhi*
Prentice-Hall of Japan, Inc., *Tokyo*
Simon & Schuster Asia Pte. Ltd., *Singapore*
Editora Prentice-Hall do Brasil, Ltda., *Rio de Janeiro*

CONTENTS

PART 3

PART 4

This is the first of four Student Books in *WORDS: Writing, Reading, Spelling*, a literacy program designed for adults and older adolescents. This program can be used in the classroom, in small groups, or one-to-one with a tutor.

Student Book One starts with the basic skills needed in developing word recognition, vocabulary, spelling, sentence writing, and reading comprehension.

Material is introduced in orderly steps; each lesson builds on the lessons that have come before it. The structured format helps learners to grasp and remember better. Continuous review is provided.

Materials for the *WORDS* program include:
- four Student Books;
- a short novel (a supplement to Student Books 3 and 4);
- a Teacher's Guide;
- Mastery Reviews for each of the four levels.

This program was developed by two teachers with many years of experience teaching adults and adolescents in the classroom and in private practice. The authors' goal is to give learners the opportunity to succeed with *words* — for writing, in reading, and for spelling.

Special note: Teachers and tutors are encouraged to refer to the program's Teacher's Guide. The Guide contains helpful background information, suggestions for introducing concepts, special multisensory teaching techniques, and all dictations.

Louise Skinner

Dianne Tucker-LaPlount

W O R D S

PART ONE

Lesson 1

The Alphabet: A Review

Read with the teacher.

The English alphabet has 26 letters.

A	B	C	D	E	F	G	H	I	J	K	L	M
N	O	P	Q	R	S	T	U	V	W	X	Y	Z

The alphabet is made up of *vowels* and *consonants*.

These letters are called **vowels:**

> A   E   I   O   U   *and   sometimes*   Y

These letters are called **consonants:**

> B   C   D   F   G   H   J   K   L   M   N   P   Q
> R   S   T   V   W   X   Z   *and   sometimes*   Y

Y can be a vowel or a consonant!

Work with the teacher.

Write the alphabet.

— — — — — — — — — — — — —

— — — — — — — — — — — — —

Write the vowels. __ __ __ __ __

Write the consonants.

— — — — — — — — — — —

— — — — — — — — — —

What letter can be a vowel or a consonant? ___

Print the correct letters on the lines.

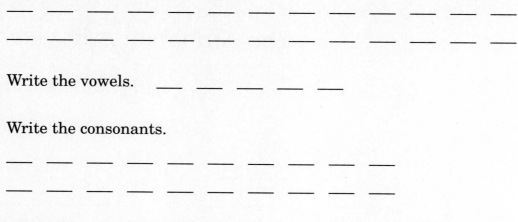

a b c ___ e f ___ h i ___ k l ___

___ o ___ ___ r s t u ___ ___ x ___ z

m n ___ p   ___ ___ ___ f

e ___ g h   ___ ___ l ___

p q ___ s   ___ f ___ ___

o ___ q r   ___ ___ h ___

w ___ y ___   ___ ___ i ___

d ___ ___ g   ___ m ___ ___

___ i ___ k   ___ ___ w ___

___ l ___ ___   ___ ___ ___ q

___ ___ d ___   ___ ___ ___ w

___ v ___ x   ___ ___ ___ v

___ ___ k ___   ___ ___ c ___

___ ___ ___ y   ___ ___ ___ m

Read with the teacher.

It is very important that you recognize the vowels and consonants.
Write the word VOWEL or CONSONANT on the line next to each letter.
Pronounce the letters for the teacher.

U ___vowel_____   u _____

x ___consonant_____   n _____

A _____   h _____

V _____   b _____

W _____   d _____

M _____   p _____

O _____   q _____

Q _____   g _____

C _____   e _____

t _____   c _____

f _____   o _____

K _____   R _____

X _____   P _____

l _____   E _____

i _____   F _____

j _____   Z _____

v _____   N _____

y _____   *(or)* _____

Each of the 16 consonants below keeps the same sound most of the time.

<pre>
    B   D   F   H   J   K   L   M   N   P   R   T   V   Z
              S   (at the beginning of a word)
              W   (at the beginning of a word)
</pre>

Read with the teacher.

The teacher will say the consonant sounds. Write the letter for each consonant sound on the line after the number.

1. _____	5. _____	9. _____	13. _____
2. _____	6. _____	10. _____	14. _____
3. _____	7. _____	11. _____	15. _____
4. _____	8. _____	12. _____	16. _____

Pronounce these words with the teacher. Write **c** under each consonant. Write **v** under each vowel.

Example: k i s s
        c v c c

1. r o t

2. i f

3. n o

4. s e e

5. h o p e

6. l u c k

7. a

8. t h a t

9. e a t

10. s t r e t c h

Do any of these words contain only consonants? The answer, of course, is *no*. Every word must have at least one vowel.

The Short Vowels: ă ĕ ĭ ŏ ŭ

Read with the teacher.

A curved mark (˘) is placed over letters which have a *short* vowel sound.

The **key words** for the short vowel sounds help you remember the sounds. The first sound of each key word is the short sound of that vowel.

THE SHORT VOWEL SOUNDS

Letter	Key Word	Sound
a	at	/ ă /
e	Ed	/ ĕ /
i	if	/ ĭ /
o	ox	/ ŏ /
u	up	/ ŭ /

Memorize these key words.

Read with the teacher.

When a vowel is followed by a consonant, the vowel is usually *short*.

Examples: at   if   up   bed   hot

A vowel plus a consonant makes a **closed syllable**. A syllable is a word or *part* of a word with one vowel sound.

Many closed syllables are small words. They have a short vowel and a consonant at the end.

This is called a VC pattern.

This is called a CVC pattern.

The words below are **closed** syllables with *short* vowel sounds. Read each word and place a curved mark (˘) over the vowel.

a	e	i	o	u
map	red	lip	job	mud
jam	let	win	top	pup
had	pen	did	not	sun
rat	web	fit	nod	nut
van	hem	kid	sob	tub
Pat	Ed	Kim	Tom	hum
Jan	Ben	Liz	Bob	Bud

Read with the teacher.

Read these closed syllable words (CVC).

bed	rut	hat	pep	fan
bad	rot	hit	pip	fin
bid	rat	hot	pop	fun
pat	ham	hut	pup	bat
pet	hem	rib	pan	bet
pit	him	rob	pen	bit
pot	hum	rub	pin	but

Write eight words by adding **b**, **f**, **h**, **m**, **p**, **r**, **s**, and **v** at the beginning of the closed syllable **at**.

1. bat   5. _____

2. fat   6. _____

3. hat   7. _____

4. _____   8. _____

Write nine words by adding **b**, **j**, **l**, **m**, **n**, **p**, **s**, **v**, and **w** at the beginning of the closed syllable **et**.

1. _____   6. _____

2. _____   7. _____

3. _____   8. _____

4. _____   9. _____

5. _____

Write seven words by adding **b, f, h, k, l, p,** and **s** at the beginning of the closed syllable **it**.

1. _____   5. _____

2. _____   6. _____

3. _____   7. _____

4. _____

Write eight words by adding **d, h, j, l, n, p, r,** and **t** at the beginning of the closed syllable **ot**.

1. _____   5. _____

2. _____   6. _____

3. _____   7. _____

4. _____   8. _____

Write four words by adding **b, h, n,** and **r** at the beginning of the closed syllable **ut**.

1. _____   3. _____

2. _____   4. _____

Write four words by adding **d, h, r,** and **v** at the beginning of the closed syllable **im**.

1. _____   3. _____

2. _____   4. _____

Write five words by adding **b, j, m, r,** and **s** at the beginning of the closed syllable **ob**.

1. _____   4. _____

2. _____   5. _____

3. _____

Work with the teacher.

On the lines next to each word, write two more words. Keep the same consonants and change only the vowels.

Example: pin _____*pan*_____ _____*pen*_____

1. ten _____ _____

2. sit _____ _____

3. rib _____ _____

4. hum _____ _____

5. hot _____ _____

6. pat _____ _____

7. lop _____ _____

8. bid _____ _____

9. but _____ _____

10. fin _____ _____

11. tap _____ _____

12. pop _____ _____

Work with the teacher.

Fill in the squares to make words going across and down.

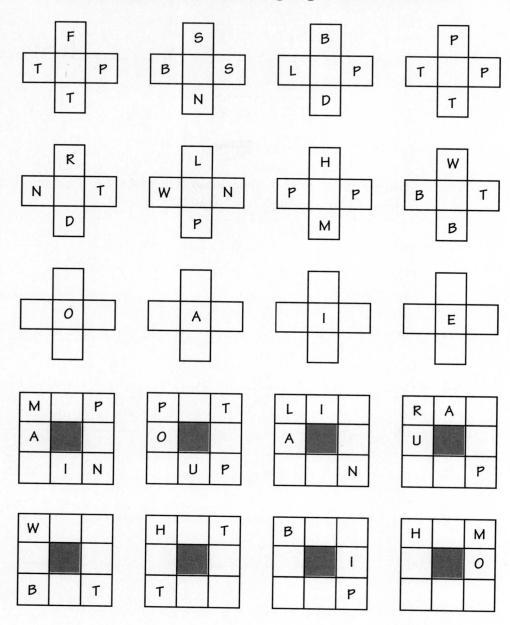

Write the vowel letter for each sound that the teacher says.

1. _____   3. _____   5. _____   7. _____

2. _____   4. _____   6. _____   8. _____

Read with the teacher.

SIGHT WORDS: THE MAVERICKS

In this book "mavericks" are words which are not pronounced the way they are spelled. You must memorize the spellings of these **sight words.**

MAVERICKS: Study these sight words with the teacher.

a	the	of
to	into	do
for	from	her

F, L, S, Z RULE

The letters **f, l, s,** and **z** are usually doubled at the end of a word with a single vowel.

Examples: puff   bell   kiss   buzz

Read the words below.

fill	doll	dull	sell
muff	miss	less	fizz
well	kill	tell	will
mess	fuss	hill	pill
fuzz	jazz	pass	fell
Jill	Jeff	Bill	Russ

Exceptions:	if	us	bus	pal

In these four words, the last letter is not doubled.

Read with the teacher.

The teacher will say one of the four words after each number. Circle the word that you hear.

1.   set   sat   sit   sot

2.   bad   bid   bed   bud

3.   pin   pan   pun   pen

4.   but   bit   bet   bat

5.   fin   fen   fan   fun

6.   hut   hot   hat   hit

7.   pop   pip   pup   pep

8.   ham   hum   hem   him

9.   pet   pit   pot   pat

10.   miss   mess   mass   muss

COMPOUND WORDS

A compound word is made by putting two small words together.

Example: sun   +   set   =   sunset

Combine the two small words to make compound words.

1. hill   +   top   =   _____

2. sun   +   tan   =   _____

3. up   +   set   =   _____

4. up   +   hill   =   _____

Read with the teacher.

Circle all the words that are the same as the one on the left.

1. sun   sumsunsnunsunnsnsunsvnsnnsunsnusumsunsunsun

2. set   satsitstsotsetsetsetsetsstsatsitsutsetsntst

3. sunset sunsetsnsetsunsatsunstsonstsunsetssntsunset

Write the **key word** for each short vowel that the teacher says.

1. _____   4. _____

2. _____   5. _____

3. _____

WORD FOCUS

Do this exercise orally with the teacher.

| sod | hem | vat | lip | buff |

(The teacher will begin with a Short Vowel Drill.)

Read with the teacher.

A syllable is a word or *part* of a word with one vowel sound.

Read the syllables below. First, point to the vowel and say its letter name. Next, say the *sound* of the vowel. Then, read the *syllable.*

1. baf	**4.** diz	**7.** fod	**10.** han	**13.** jez
2. ket	**5.** lum	**8.** nib	**11.** med	**14.** rup
3. pov	**6.** zog	**9.** tep	**12.** suf	**15.** lav

Listen, then circle the syllable that the teacher says. Pay special attention to the vowel sound. Start with row 1.

1.	fib	fab	feb	**4.**	maf	mof	muf
2.	pom	pem	pim	**5.**	niz	nez	naz
3.	sil	sel	sul	**6.**	vit	vut	vot

The teacher will dictate three syllables.

1. _____   2. _____   3. _____

Work with the teacher.

Read each numbered sentence below and answer the questions.
Write each answer in sentence form, underlining the exact word or
words that answer the question. The first two are done for you.

1. Jeff had a map in his van.

   a. Who had a map in his van?

   <u>Jeff</u> had a map in his van.

   b. Where did Jeff have a map?

   Jeff had a map <u>in his van.</u>

   c. Jeff had what in his van?

   _____

2. Pat met the vet at the lab.

   a. Who met the vet at the lab?

   _____

   b. Pat met whom at the lab?

   _____

   c. Pat met the vet where?

   _____

3. The pup bit the man on the lip.

    a. The pup bit the man where?

    _____

    b. What bit the man on the lip?

    _____

    c. The pup bit whom on the lip?

    _____

Complete these sentences in your own words.

1. The men hid the map _____ .
                                            (where?)

2. Ron _____ the man in a hut on a hill.
                (did what?)

3. _____ fed the hen.
        (who?)

WORDS

_____   _____

_____   _____

_____   _____

_____   _____

_____   _____

_____   _____

_____   _____

WORD GROUPS

_____

_____

_____

_____

_____

SENTENCES

_____

_____

_____

_____

The Long Vowels: ā ē ī ō ū

Read with the teacher.

A vowel is *long* when it sounds like its name in the alphabet. A short line (¯) is placed over a letter when it has a long vowel sound.

The **key words** for the long vowel sounds are given below.

THE LONG VOWEL SOUNDS

Letter Pattern	Key Word	Sound
a _ e	safe	/ ā /
e _ e	eve	/ ē /
i _ e	dime	/ ī /
o _ e	vote	/ ō /
u _ e	mule	/ ū /
	rule	/ o͞o /

This is a CVCe pattern.

consonant vowel consonant ¯ e

l   i   f   e

Read with the teacher.

If a word ends with the letter **e**, the **e** is usually silent. It is not pronounced.

One of the main functions of the silent **e** is to change the sound of the first vowel in the word.

Examples: nŏt *changes to* nōte
   hăt *changes to* hāte
   dĭm *changes to* dīme

The silent **e** has caused the first vowel in **note, hate,** and **dime** to have the long vowel sound.

Read these words with the class or teacher. Place a line (ˉ) over each long vowel.

sake	time	mile	rave	size
fake	lime	tile	wave	side
take	line	fine	save	wide
lake	joke	vine	safe	wife
make	poke	bone	rude	life
male	pike	lone	rule	live *
mule	like	tone	wire	five
mole	hike	tune	fire	eve

---

* The word **live** can be pronounced / līv / or / lĭv /. See the sight words on the following page. Each pronunciation has a different meaning.

Read with the teacher.

If a silent **e** is at the end of a one-syllable word, the first vowel in the word will almost always have the long sound.

The teacher will dictate words which have *short* vowel sounds. On the first line, write the word that is dictated. On the line next to it, write the word again. Then, add an **e**. Pronounce the new word.

Example: _____ not _____   _____ note _____

1. ___ kit ___ _____   10. _____ _____

2. _____ _____   11. _____ _____

3. _____ _____   12. _____ _____

4. _____ _____   13. _____ _____

5. _____ _____   14. _____ _____

6. _____ _____   15. _____ _____

7. _____ _____   16. _____ _____

8. _____ _____   17. _____ _____

9. _____ _____   18. _____ _____

MAVERICKS: Study these sight words with the teacher.

one	**have**	**done**	**move**
some	**love**	**come**	**live ***

---

* The sight word **live** is pronounced / lĭv /.

Read with the teacher.

Write seven words by adding **b, f, l, m, r, t,** and **w** at the beginning of the syllable **ake**.

1. _____bake_____   5. _____

2. _____fake_____   6. _____

3. _____   7. _____

4. _____

Write eight words by adding **d, f, l, m, n, p, v,** and **w** at the beginning of the syllable **ine**.

1. _____   5. _____

2. _____   6. _____

3. _____   7. _____

4. _____   8. _____

Write four words by adding **f, h, t,** and **w** at the beginning of the syllable **ire**.

1. _____   3. _____

2. _____   4. _____

Write six words by adding **b, h, m, p, s,** and **t** at the beginning of the syllable **ale**.

1. _____   4. _____

2. _____   5. _____

3. _____   6. _____

Write three words by adding **h, m,** and **r** at the beginning of the syllable **ope**.

1. _____   3. _____

2. _____

Work with the teacher.

Fill in the squares to make words going across and down. Each word should end with an **e**.

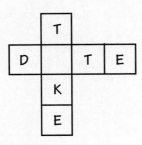
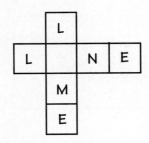

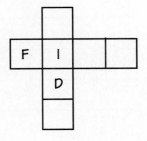
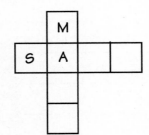
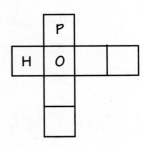

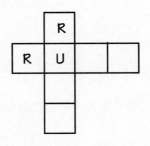
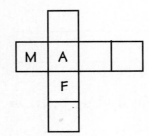
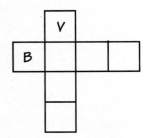

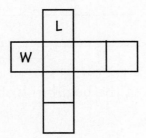

The Long Vowels

Read with the teacher.

Write **L** if the first vowel in the word is *long*. Write **S** if it is *short*.

Examples: hat __S__   dime __L__

1. ate _____
2. lop _____
3. tile _____
4. rake _____
5. bell _____
6. rut _____
7. home _____
8. side _____
9. tin _____
10. tame _____

11. jam _____
12. huff _____
13. eve _____
14. wit _____
15. wife _____
16. pun _____
17. fizz _____
18. rude _____
19. tan _____
20. set _____

MAVERICKS: Study these sight words with the teacher.

are	were	here

Fill in each blank with the correct letter.

are	*were*	*here*
a ___ e	w e r ___	h ___ r e
a r ___	w ___ r ___	h ___ r ___
___ r e	___ e ___ e	___ e r ___
___ ___ e	___ ___ ___ e	___ ___ ___ e
___ ___ ___	___ ___ ___ ___	___ ___ ___ ___

Read with the teacher.

Make compound words.

1. bed + side = _____

2. life + time = _____

3. fire + man = _____

4. home + made = _____

5. in + side = _____

6. make + up = _____

7. bed + time = _____

8. hill + side = _____

MORE ABOUT THE SILENT E

Some common words have a silent **e** immediately following a vowel.

This is a CVe pattern.

t i e   s e e   d u e

There is no consonant letter between the vowel that you hear and the silent **e**. The silent **e** has caused the first vowel to have a long sound.

Copy these words. Pronounce them with the class or teacher.

1. doe _____   5. fee _____

2. hoe _____   6. pie _____

3. foe _____   7. die _____

4. sue _____   8. lie _____

Read with the teacher.

Some words have only one vowel with no consonant after it. The vowel is usually long.

Examples: be he me we no so I

(Notice that *I* by itself is always a capital letter.)

Read these sentences with the class or teacher.

1. Joe will take a jet from Nome to Rome.

2. I hope the jet will be here on time.

3. Sue and I were late.

4. We were due on the job at nine.

5. Did Lee vote for the men?

6. He did not vote for one man.

7. The vote was a tie.

8. The vet wore a red tie.

9. He will see the pet at five.

10. The lab fee will be $20.

11. We like to lie in the sun.

12. Did he tell me a lie?

WORD FOCUS

Do this exercise orally with the teacher.

lop	lope	fame	jute

(The teacher will begin with a Short and Long Vowel Drill.)

Read with the teacher.

Read the syllables below. First, say the letters in the VCe pattern and point to the first vowel, the consonant, and the silent **e**. Next, say the *sound* of the first vowel. Then, read the *syllable.*

1. nate	**4.** dole	**7.** fute	**10.** pune	**13.** lete
2. bine	**5.** vade	**8.** vite	**11.** node	**14.** fide
3. pede	**6.** zone	**9.** tize	**12.** hale	**15.** ruke

Listen, then circle the syllable that the teacher says. Start with row 1.

1.	nide	nade	nede	**5.**	mafe	mofe	mife
2.	lome	leme	lume	**6.**	nize	nuze	naze
3.	zile	zale	zule	**7.**	jite	jute	jate
4.	fibe	fabe	fobe	**8.**	rave	rove	rive

The teacher will dictate three syllables.

1. _____   2. _____   3. _____

Work with the teacher.

Read each numbered sentence below and answer the questions. Write each answer in sentence form, underlining the exact word or words that answer the question. The first two are done for you.

1. The bell woke Wade at five.

   a. What woke Wade at five?

      <u>The bell</u> woke Wade at five.

   b. When did the bell wake Wade?

      The bell woke Wade <u>at five</u>.

   c. What did the bell do to Wade at five?

      _____

   d. The bell woke whom at five?

      _____

2. The doe ran to the lake.

   a. Where did the doe run?

      _____

   b. What ran to the lake?

      _____

Complete these sentences in your own words.

1. Pete will take _____ to Rome.
                           (whom or what?)

2. Five men _____ the homemade pie.
                (did what?)

DICTATION

WORDS

_____   _____

_____   _____

_____   _____

_____   _____

_____   _____

_____   _____

_____   _____

WORD GROUPS

_____

_____

_____

_____

_____

SENTENCES

_____

_____

_____

_____

A Review of Short and Long Vowels

Read with the teacher.

Write **L** if the first vowel in the word is *long*. Write **S** if it is *short*.

Examples: hat ___S___   dime ___L___

1. bet	_____	**13.** June	_____
2. doze	_____	**14.** hut	_____
3. dim	_____	**15.** eve	_____
4. mute	_____	**16.** lube	_____
5. jet	_____	**17.** jot	_____
6. rake	_____	**18.** lope	_____
7. sit	_____	**19.** tune	_____
8. dud	_____	**20.** pup	_____
9. nod	_____	**21.** den	_____
10. dole	_____	**22.** rid	_____
11. take	_____	**23.** duke	_____
12. fade	_____	**24.** nape	_____

Read these words with the class or teacher.

tap	pane	rat
tape	pan	rate
van	kit	mate
vane	kite	mat
hop	rob	hide
hope	robe	hid
pal	fine	man
pale	fin	mane
fate	win	pet
fat	wine	Pete
mope	rid	dime
mop	ride	dim
Jan	rode	rip
Jane	rod	ripe
ate	us	tube
at	use	tub

Read with the teacher.

The letters **f, l, s,** and **z** are usually doubled at the end of a word with one vowel. However, there are some exceptions (see page 11).

Read these sentences with the class or teacher. Underline the exceptions.

1. A <u>pal</u> of mine had a pass to ride the <u>bus</u>.

2. Jill will tell us if the bell woke Russ.

3. If the bus is late, will Jeff take the van?

Work with the teacher.

Fill in each blank with the correct word.

1. Five men _____ in the den.
   sat   sate

2. Dave had a _____ time at the lake.
   fin   fine

3. I _____ Bob will come home on time.
   hop   hope

4. Pat _____ the note in the safe.
   hid   hide

5. Did the pup _____ the man on the toe?
   bit   bite

6. The _____ ran into a hole.
   rat   rate

7. I _____ some of the ham in the pan.
   at   ate

8. Pete _____ the bus to the mill.
   rod   rode

Read with the teacher.

Circle at least 15 words, both across and down.

J O K E F A T M O M

U T A P P B H O M E

N O T E H A T P A N

E N Z Z I P B O N E

E E L A K E U K I T

E W A V E N T E V E

WORD LIST

bone	man
but	men
eve	mom
fat	mop
hat	note
hike	pan
home	poke
joke	tap
June	tone
kit	wave
lake	zip

The teacher will dictate 20 words.

1. _____
2. _____
3. _____
4. _____
5. _____
6. _____
7. _____
8. _____
9. _____
10. _____

11. _____
12. _____
13. _____
14. _____
15. _____
16. _____
17. _____
18. _____
19. _____
20. _____

A Review of Short and Long Vowels

PART TWO

The Sounds of the Letter **s**

Read with the teacher.

At the beginning of a word, the letter **s** has the sound / s /.

sun	safe	same
set	sale	save
sad	sake	side

After a long vowel, the letter **s** usually has the sound / z /.

wise	rose	rise
nose	fuse	hose
use *		

MAVERICK: Study this sight word with the teacher.

was

---

* The **s** in **use** can be pronounced / s / or / z /. Each pronunciation has a different meaning.

Read with the teacher.

The letter **s** is usually doubled at the end of a word with one short vowel. (This spelling pattern was given in Lesson 2.)

kiss   mess   fuss

However, a few words are spelled with only one **s**. In the words below, the **s** may sound like / s / or / z /. You will have to memorize these words.

as	**us**	**his**
is	**has**	**bus**

Use the dictionary to find the *pronunciation* of these words. The teacher will explain how to do this.

1. as   ăz _____   4. has _____

2. is   _____   5. his _____

3. us   _____   6. bus _____

Fill in each blank with the correct word.

1. I will save $500 if I _____ the van on June 10.
                        sale   sell

2. The _____ of five and five is ten.
        sun   sum

3. The pup hid _____ bone in a mole hole.
                his   him

4. Is it a _____ to tell a lie?
            sill   sin

5. Has Ann gone to the _____ ?
                        sale   sell

6. Did Ed _____ his pass on the bus?
            use   us

Read with the teacher.

In the middle of a word, after a short vowel, the letter **s** *usually* has the sound of / s /.

ba<u>s</u>ket   si<u>s</u>ter   le<u>ss</u>on   ma<u>s</u>ter

Write **S** if the **s** sounds like / s /. Write **Z** if the **s** sounds like / z /.
Pronounce the words with the class or teacher.

Example: sun <u>S</u>   nose <u>Z</u>

1. save   _____   8. safe   _____

2. hose   _____   9. wise   _____

3. sister   _____   10. sad   _____

4. as   _____   11. was   _____

5. us   _____   12. rose   _____

6. fuse   _____   13. bus   _____

7. is   _____   14. basket   _____

WORD FOCUS

Do this exercise orally with the teacher.

| fuss | fuse | sip | site |

(The teacher will begin with a Short and Long Vowel Drill.)

Read with the teacher.

First, point to the vowel and say its letter name. Next, say the *sound* of the vowel. Then, read the *syllable.*

1.	bon	**6.**	jav	**11.**	kel	**16.**	vit
2.	sim	**7.**	hep	**12.**	sav	**17.**	suz
3.	mep	**8.**	sib	**13.**	zan	**18.**	dub
4.	sut	**9.**	dop	**14.**	jum	**19.**	rom
5.	lud	**10.**	sef	**15.**	sep	**20.**	wid

Listen, then circle the syllable that the teacher says.

1.	jid	jad	jud	jod	**6.**	sev	sav	suv	sov
2.	fip	fup	fep	fop	**7.**	vut	vat	vot	vet
3.	nul	nil	nol	nel	**8.**	zim	zem	zam	zom
4.	dif	daf	dof	duf	**9.**	ron	run	rin	ren
5.	miz	maz	moz	mez	**10.**	tib	tab	teb	tob

The teacher will dictate three syllables.

1. _____ 2. _____ 3. _____

Work with the teacher.

Read each numbered sentence below and answer the questions. Write each answer in sentence form, underlining the word or words that answer the question.

1. Russ rode his bike to the lake.

    a. Where did Russ ride his bike?

        <u>Russ rode his bike to the lake.</u>

    b. What did Russ ride to the lake?

        _____

    c. Who rode his bike to the lake?

        _____

2. Sue woke up at sunrise.

    a. Who woke up at sunrise?

        _____

    b. When did Sue wake up?

        _____

    c. What did Sue do at sunrise?

        _____

Complete these sentences in your own words.

1. The sad man _____ on the red bus.
                      (did what?)

2. Sam will take his pill _____ .
                              (when?)

DICTATION

WORDS

_____   _____

_____   _____

_____   _____

_____   _____

_____   _____

_____   _____

_____   _____

WORD GROUPS

_____

_____

_____

_____

_____

SENTENCES

_____

_____

_____

_____

The Sounds of the Letter **y**

Read with the teacher.

When is <u>y</u> a consonant? The letter **y** is a consonant when it is the first letter of a word.

yes	yam	yap	yule
yet	yak	yell	yuletide

MAVERICKS: Study these sight words with the teacher.

you	your

When is <u>y</u> a vowel? The letter **y** is a vowel when it takes the place of a long or short **i** within a word.

Examples: type   / ī /   gym   / ĭ /

The letter **y** also is a vowel when it takes the place of a long **i** or long **e** at the end of a word.

Examples: my   / ī /   happy   / ē /

Read with the teacher.

Copy these words. Pronounce them with the class or teacher.

1. by   _____
2. baby   _____
3. July   _____
4. dye   _____

5. lady   _____
6. rye   _____
7. nylon   _____
8. navy   _____

MAVERICKS: Study these sight words with the teacher.

buy	money	eye

Write CONSONANT if the **y** is a consonant. Write VOWEL if the **y** is a vowel.

Examples: nylon   _vowel_____

           yes   _consonant_____

1. yell   _____
2. baby   _____
3. type   _____
4. July   _____
5. yam   _____
6. lady   _____
7. yak   _____
8. happy   _____

9. you   _____
10. rye   _____
11. by   _____
12. navy   _____
13. yule   _____
14. yet   _____
15. my   _____
16. yen   _____

Read with the teacher.

Fill in each blank with the correct letter.

buy

b ___ y

b u ___

b ___ ___

___ ___ y

___ ___ ___

you

y o ___

y ___ u

___ ___ u

y ___ ___

___ ___ ___

eye

e ___ e

___ y e

e y ___

e ___ ___

___ ___ ___

your

___ o u r

___ o ___ r

y ___ u ___

___ ___ ___ r

___ ___ ___ ___

money

m ___ n ___ y

m ___ n ___ ___

___ ___ ___ e y

___ ___ ___ ___ y

___ ___ ___ ___ ___

Read these sentences with the class or teacher.

1. Has Russ come home yet? Did you see him?
2. Your van is due for a tune-up.
3. Will a yam rot in the hot sun?
4. I like ham on rye. Do you?
5. Yes, I will type a note to the lady in the lab.
6. Tell Pat to buy some nylon hose for her mom.
7. The men at the mill like to yak a lot.
8. Dee will dye her robe red.
9. The man has a sty on the lid of his eye.
10. Did Lynn make a lot of money at her sale?

Circle all the words that are the same as the one on the left.

1. **July**   JullyJulJulyJulvJulvJullyJulyJulyJolyJullvJuly

2. **you**   yuoyouyouyouyoyuovouvuoynoyuyououuouyuyoyouyou

WORD FOCUS

Do this exercise orally with the teacher.

yon	lye	yip

(The teacher will begin with a Short and Long Vowel Drill.)

Read with the teacher.

First, point to the vowel or VCe pattern and say the letter or letters. Next, say the *sound* of the vowel. Then, read the *syllable*.

1. yit		**5.** yif		**9.** yav		**13.** dyne		**17.** lyze
2. sys		**6.** yep		**10.** bys		**14.** ryle		**18.** zyme
3. yab		**7.** dys		**11.** lym		**15.** tyne		**19.** pyle
4. nym		**8.** yop		**12.** yup		**16.** nype		**20.** bype

Listen, then circle the syllable that the teacher says.

1. yin	yan	yen	yun		**6.** sib	sab	sub	seb
2. vez	vaz	viz	voz		**7.** yup	yep	yip	yop
3. wib	web	wub	wob		**8.** buf	bif	baf	bof
4. zik	zek	zok	zak		**9.** pib	peb	pob	pab
5. fid	fed	fud	fod		**10.** kal	kul	kol	kel

The teacher will dictate three syllables.

1. _____   **2.** _____   **3.** _____

SENTENCE FOCUS

Work with the teacher.

Read each numbered sentence below and answer the questions. Write each answer in sentence form, underlining the exact word or words that answer the question.

1. Jan will type my note at home.

    a. Who will type my note at home?

    _____

    b. Jan will type what at home?

    _____

    c. Where will Jan type my note?

    _____

2. Kyle will take the jet at five.

    a. When will Kyle take the jet?

    _____

    b. Who will take the jet at five?

    _____

    c. What will Kyle take at five?

    _____

Complete these sentences in your own words.

1. The baby ate _____ .
                              (what?)

2. _____ met his wife by the lake.
      (who?)

DICTATION

WORDS

_____   _____

_____   _____

_____   _____

_____   _____

_____   _____

_____   _____

_____   _____

WORD GROUPS

_____

_____

_____

_____

_____

SENTENCES

_____

_____

_____

_____

The Sounds of **q** and **x**

THE LETTER Q

Read with the teacher.

The letter **q** has no sound of its own. In English words, the letter **u** *always* comes after **q**. Together, **qu** sounds like / kw /.

Example: quiz *sounds like* / kwĭz /

Do not pronounce the **u** as a vowel. It may help you to think of the **u** as separate from the vowel that comes after it.

Examples: qu it   qu ite   qu ake

Copy these words. Mark the vowels that you *hear*. Place a short line over each long vowel. Place a curved line over each short vowel.

REMEMBER: The **u** after **q** is silent. The **e** at the end of a word is also silent.

1. quite ____quīte____   4. quake _____

2. quit _____   5. quiz _____

3. quote _____   6. quip _____

Read these sentences with the class or teacher.

1. Lee has made quite a lot of money.

2. I hate to take a quiz!

3. Is it time to quit?

4. He did not quote a fee for the job.

5. My quip made Sue mad.

6. The quake woke us up.

Read with the teacher.

Fill in each blank with the correct word.

1. My eye is sore and _____ red.
   quit   quite

2. The man at the jet lab _____ his job.
   quit   quite

3. Did Tom pass the _____ ?
   quip   quiz

4. A *joke* is the same as a _____ .
   quote   quip

5. His wife is _____ ill.
   quite   quake

Exception:	Iraq

This is not an English word.

Read with the teacher.

The letter **x** usually sounds like / ks /.

Example: box *sounds like* / boks /

Read these words with the class or teacher.

ax	six	tax	fox	fix
ox	tux	mix	wax	fax

Fill in each blank with a word from the list above.

1. It will take _____ men to do the job.

2. The _____ ran from the men and hid in his den.

3. Did Max _____ the hose in his van?

4. The _____ on my home is due in July.

Circle all the words that are the same as the one on the left.

1. tax textxtaxtuxfaxtaxtatxtuxtxtextaxtaxtixtoxtxtaxtax

2. wax wxmaxwixwexwuxwaxmaxmixxawxwaxwoxwaxwixwexwexwaxx

Circle at least 10 words, both across and down.

Q	U	A	K	E	B	O	X	Q
U	X	F	I	X	Z	X	R	U
I	M	O	Q	U	O	T	E	I
T	A	X	M	I	X	U	H	T
E	Q	U	I	Z	A	X	O	T

WORD LIST

ax	quake
box	quit
fix	quite
fox	quiz
mix	quote
ox	tax
	tux

Read these word groups with the class or teacher.

fax the note to him

if you take the quiz

has quit his job

will quote the note

the ox and the mule

will use an ax

the size of the tux

if the tax is due

was quite upset

WORD FOCUS

Do this exercise orally with the teacher.

quite	quit	lox	pyx

(The teacher will begin with a Short and Long Vowel Drill.)

Read with the teacher.

First, point to the vowel or VCe pattern and say the letter or letters. Next, say the *sound* of the vowel. Then, read the *syllable.*

1. quib	**5.** nux	**9.** quel	**13.** quipe	**17.** quede
2. nox	**6.** quin	**10.** lux	**14.** quone	**18.** quine
3. bax	**7.** lex	**11.** quid	**15.** quate	**19.** quoke
4. ques	**8.** quip	**12.** tox	**16.** quade	**20.** quire

Listen, then circle the syllable that the teacher says.

1. quem	quom	quam	quim	**6.**	nix	nax	nux	nex
2. yit	yat	yut	yot	**7.**	yib	yab	yob	yub
3. nex	nux	nox	nax	**8.**	quoz	quiz	quaz	quex
4. yod	yed	yid	yad	**9.**	yif	yef	yaf	yof
5. quev	quov	quiv	quav	**10.**	quop	quep	quip	quap

The teacher will dictate three syllables.

1. _____ 2. _____ 3. _____

Work with the teacher.

Look at the grid below. Read and discuss the headings. Each heading covers a part of a sentence. Read the following sentences and insert them in the grid. The first two have been done for you.

1. Tex quit his job.
2. A fox ate the hen.
3. Max fed the ox.
4. Lyn hid the quiz.

SUBJECT	VERB	OBJECT
Who? (or What?)	*Did?*	*What?*
Tex	quit	his job.
A fox	ate	the hen.

WORDS

_____   _____

_____   _____

_____   _____

_____   _____

_____   _____

_____   _____

_____   _____

WORD GROUPS

_____

_____

_____

_____

_____

SENTENCES

_____

_____

_____

_____

The Sounds of the Letter **c**

Read with the teacher.

> The letter **c** will sound like / s /
> if **e** , **i** , or **y** comes after the **c**.

$$
\mathbf{c} \left\langle \begin{array}{l} \mathbf{e} \\ \mathbf{i} \\ \mathbf{y} \end{array} \right. \quad = \quad / \,s\, /
$$

This letter is called the **soft c**.

Examples: / s / / s / / s /
   cell   city   cycle

If the **c** is followed by *any other letter* or *no letter at all*, it almost always has a / k / sound.

This letter is called the **hard c**.

Examples: / k / / k / / k /
   cat   cop   talc_

> **Exception:**   soccer

Read with the teacher.

Write **S** if the letter **c** sounds like / s /. Write **K** if the letter **c** sounds like / k /. Then pronounce the words with the class or teacher.

1. cot   <u>   K   </u>

2. cuff   _____

3. nice   _____

4. cave   _____

5. cove   _____

6. case   _____

7. cite   _____

8. ace   _____

9. ice   _____

10. cell   _____

11. cone   _____

12. can   _____

13. race   _____

14. rice   _____

15. cab   _____

16. cob   _____

17. mice   _____

18. lace   _____

19. cure   _____

20. pace   _____

21. came   _____

22. since   _____

23. fence   _____

24. dance   _____

Compare these words.

cut	cub	can
cute	cube	cane
cop	cap	cod
cope	cape	code

Read with the teacher.

Make compound words.

1. can + not = _____

2. cup + cake = _____

3. hub + cap = _____

4. cat + nap = _____

5. cob + web = _____

Read these sentences with the class or teacher.

1. A cop will cite you if you pass on a hill.

2. Did you take a cab to the dance?

3. Since Cal has a cut on his toe, he will not run in the race.

4. Some mice were in the box of cake mix.

5. Let me have an ice cube for my 7-Up.

6. Do you have a job in the city?

7. A fat cat ate some cod by the cove.

8. Cy has not had a date since he came to Cape Cod.

9. Will a pill cure my sore eye?

10. In case you cannot come, I will save some cake for you.

11. Do you like soccer?

12. Did Dale fix the hole in the fence yet?

13. Rod has a bad cut on his face.

14. My zip code is 51696 — five, one, six, nine, six.

Work with the teacher.

CROSSWORD PUZZLE: Fill in each blank with a vowel to make words across and down.

C		L	L	▓	▓	▓	▓	C
	▓		▓		C	E	▓	
R		C	E	▓		▓		P
E	▓	E	▓		N		C	E
▓	S		F	▓	▓	C	▓	▓
R		C		▓		E	▓	C
▓	N		N		C	▓	▓	
▓	C		C		▓		▓	T
▓	E		E		P		C	E

REVIEW

The letter **c** will sound like _____ if the

letter _____ , _____ , or _____ comes after the **c**.

WORD FOCUS

Do this exercise orally with the teacher.

cod	code	cyme	lice

(The teacher will begin with a Short and Long Vowel Drill.)

Read with the teacher.

First, point to the vowel or VCe pattern and say the letter or letters. Next, say the *sound* of the vowel. Then, read the *syllable*.

1. cid	**5.** cipe	**9.** ceve	**13.** cud	**17.** cabe
2. cede	**6.** cam	**10.** ceb	**14.** tic	**18.** quice
3. vac	**7.** fice	**11.** vice	**15.** cyme	**19.** cen
4. tice	**8.** cobe	**12.** dace	**16.** sec	**20.** cyt

Listen, then circle the syllable that the teacher says.

1.	mete	mite	mote	mate
2.	sume	same	sime	seme
3.	lide	lode	lede	lude
4.	dane	dine	dune	dene
5.	bole	bale	bile	bule
6.	vipe	vope	vepe	vape
7.	nume	name	nime	nome
8.	pace	pice	poce	pece

The teacher will dictate three syllables.

1. _____   2. _____   3. _____

Work with the teacher.

Read the following sentences and insert them in the grid. The first one has been done for you.

1. Cal cut the pie.

2. A cab hit the van.

3. The cub bit my cat.

4. Mice ate the cake.

SUBJECT	VERB	OBJECT
Who? (or What?)	*Did?*	*What?*
Cal	cut	the pie.

DICTATION

WORDS

_____   _____

_____   _____

_____   _____

_____   _____

_____   _____

_____   _____

_____   _____

WORD GROUPS

_____

_____

_____

_____

_____

SENTENCES

_____

_____

_____

_____

_____

The Sounds of the Letter **g**

Read with the teacher.

> The letter **g** will sound like / j /
> if **e** , **i** , or **y** comes after the **g**.

g ⟨ e
    i = / j /
    y

This letter is called the **soft g**.

Examples: / j /   / j /   / j /
             gem   gin   gym

If the **g** is followed by *any other letter* or *no letter at all*, it usually has a / g / sound.

This letter is called the **hard g**.

Examples: / g /   / g /   / g /
             go   gun   mug_

Read with the teacher.

Write **J** if the letter **g** sounds like / j /. Write **G** if the letter **g** sounds like / g /. Then pronounce the words with the class or teacher.

1. gum	_____G_____	13. pig _____
2. gem	_____	14. dig _____
3. age	_____	15. big _____
4. gas	_____	16. beg _____
5. sag	_____	17. bag _____
6. hinge	_____	18. bug _____
7. hug	_____	19. gyp _____
8. huge	_____	20. singe _____
9. gym	_____	21. gaze _____
10. gag	_____	22. gull _____
11. page	_____	23. leg _____
12. got	_____	24. gate _____

Pronounce these words with the class or teacher.

game	hug	rage	cage
gyp	huge	rag	sag
bag	gaze	age	gate
gun	gem	singe	lunge
wage	jug	gull	gut
wag	wig	gin	keg

Work with the teacher.

Follow the directions. After writing each new word, say it out loud.

1. Write the word **rag**. _____

2. Add *e* to the end of the word **rag**. _____

3. Change the *r* to *w*. _____

4. Take away the *e*. _____

5. Change the *w* to *g*. _____

6. Change the last *g* to *m*. _____

7. Change the *a* to *e*. _____

8. Change the *e* to *y*. _____

9. Change the *m* to *p*. _____

10. Change the *y* to *a*. _____

11. Change the *g* to *r*. _____

12. Change the *p* to *g*. _____

MAVERICK: Study this sight word with the teacher.

gone

Circle all the words that are the same as the one on the left.

1. **gum** gungumqumgungnungumgungungunqunqumguwumgmugum

2. **big** begdigbiqbiqbigbegbjgigjiqbjgbigbiqdigbigbiqg

Read with the teacher.

Circle at least 15 words, both across and down.

R   A   G   E   M   M   U   G

I   R   E   Z   P   I   G   O

G   A   M   E   R   I   G   T

G   G   G   G   U   N   O   H

U   Y   S   A   G   I   N   U

M   P   A   G   E   H   U   G

G   A   Z   E   C   A   G   E

WORD LIST	
cage	huge
gag	mug
game	page
gaze	pig
gem	rag
got	rage
gum	rig
gun	rug
hug	sag

REVIEW

The letter **g** will sound like _____ if the

letter _____ , _____ , or _____ comes after the **g**.

Exceptions to the *g* rule:

get   give   girl   gift   begin

There are some exceptions to the **g** rule. Each of the words in the box above has the letter **g** followed by an **e** or an **i**, but the **g** in these words does not sound like /j/. The **g** keeps its hard /g/ sound.

Copy the words in the box and memorize them.

1. _____   4. _____

2. _____   5. _____

3. _____

Read with the teacher.

Fill in the blanks to complete each sentence. Use the words from the list.

1. Did you go to the game at the g_____ ?

2. The bike race will b_____ on time.

3. Liz gave her dad a big h_____ and kiss.

4. Bob will fix the h_____ on the g_____ .

5. Did Gene give his g_____ a g_____ .

6. The sale at the car lot was a big g_____ ?

7. The h_____ p_____ was in his pen.

8. Meg has gone to get some g_____ for the van.

WORD LIST
begin
gas
gate
gift
girl
gym
gyp
hinge
hug
huge
pig

REVIEW

Five common words that are exceptions to the **g** rule are

_____ , _____ , _____ , _____ , and _____ .

WORD FOCUS

Do this exercise orally with the teacher.

fig	sage	gap	gibe

(The teacher will begin with a Short and Long Vowel Drill.)

Read with the teacher.

First, point to the vowel or VCe pattern and say the letter or letters. Next, say the *sound* of the vowel. Then, read the *syllable*.

1. gen	**5.** nage	**9.** cym	**13.** gid	**17.** gac
2. gace	**6.** gup	**10.** luge	**14.** col	**18.** gabe
3. cim	**7.** gyze	**11.** quig	**15.** gope	**19.** gic
4. gub	**8.** cax	**12.** gade	**16.** gyn	**20.** fuge

Listen, then circle the syllable that the teacher says.

1.	boz	beze	bez	biz	**6.**	tev	tiv	tive	teve
2.	nup	nupe	nop	nep	**7.**	fin	fen	fone	fon
3.	quib	queb	quab	quabe	**8.**	sime	sim	sem	sume
4.	pob	pub	pobe	pib	**9.**	vit	vot	vite	vut
5.	yite	yote	yute	yut	**10.**	wiv	wuv	wove	wov

The teacher will dictate three syllables.

1. _____ **2.** _____ **3.** _____

SENTENCE FOCUS

Work with the teacher.

Read the following sentences and insert them in the grid. The first one has been done for you. (Note that the heading "Where?" has been added to the grid.)

1. The pig dug a hole in the pen.

2. The girl set the vase on the sill.

3. Gene got a ride to the gym.

4. The man hid the gun in a bag.

5. Gus rode his bike to the lake.

6. Pam met Gabe at the game.

SUBJECT	VERB	OBJECT	
Who? (or What?)	**Did?**	**What? (or Whom?)**	**Where?**
The pig	dug	a hole	in the pen.

DICTATION

WORDS

_____   _____

_____   _____

_____   _____

_____   _____

_____   _____

_____   _____

_____   _____

WORD GROUPS

_____

_____

_____

_____

_____

SENTENCES

_____

_____

_____

_____

Review

Read with the teacher.

Fill in the blanks to complete the rule about the sound of the letter **c**.

The letter **c** will sound like _____ if the

letter _____ , _____ , or _____ comes after the **c**.

Read these words. If the **c** sounds like /s/, write **S** on the line after each word below. If the **c** sounds like /k/, write **K** on the line.

1. ice _____   6. mice _____   11. since _____

2. cub _____   7. cuff _____   12. can _____

3. pace _____   8. fence _____   13. cope _____

4. cone _____   9. city _____   14. dance _____

5. cite _____   10. cell _____   15. came _____

Listen, then circle the word that the teacher says.

1.	bed	bad	bud	bid
2.	pot	pat	pit	pet
3.	pun	pen	pin	pan
4.	dill	dell	dull	doll
5.	hot	hat	hit	hut
6.	him	hem	ham	hum
7.	rib	rob	robe	rub
8.	pop	pup	pep	pip
9.	let	lot	lit	late
10.	mass	mess	muss	miss
11.	cut	cute	cub	cube
12.	cap	cop	cope	cape
13.	cane	can	came	cam
14.	fan	fine	fun	fin
15.	game	gem	gym	gam

Fill in the blanks to complete the rule about the sound of the letter **g**.

> The letter **g** will sound like _____ if the
>
> letter _____ , _____ , or _____ comes after the **g**.

Read with the teacher.

Read these words. If the **g** sounds like /j/, write **J** on the line after each word below. If the **g** sounds like /g/, write **G** on the line.

1. bug _____
2. gym _____
3. age _____
4. gate _____
5. got _____

6. page _____
7. gag _____
8. gin _____
9. gem _____
10. gum _____

11. gull _____
12. rage _____
13. lunge _____
14. gone _____
15. singe _____

Five common words do not follow the rule about the sound of **g**. They are *exceptions* to the rule. Write those words on the lines below. (See page 63, Lesson 9.)

_____ _____ _____ _____ _____

Read these words. If the **s** sounds like /s/, write **S** on the line after each word below. If the **s** sounds like /z/, write **Z** on the line.

1. fuss _____
2. sell _____
3. his _____

4. sale _____
5. use _____
6. us _____

7. bus _____
8. rose _____
9. mess _____

Read with the teacher.

Write the vowel letter which is the same as the sound that you hear.

1. _____ 2. _____ 3. _____ 4. _____ 5. _____ 6. _____

What letter can be either a vowel or a consonant? _____

The teacher will say a short vowel sound after each number below. Write the <u>key</u> <u>word</u> for each short vowel sound that you hear.

1. _____ 4. _____

2. _____ 5. _____

3. _____

The teacher will dictate 14 words.

1. _____ 8. _____

2. _____ 9. _____

3. _____ 10. _____

4. _____ 11. _____

5. _____ 12. _____

6. _____ 13. _____

7. _____ 14. _____

PART THREE

Lesson 11

Beginning Consonant Blends

Read with the teacher.

A consonant blend is made up of two or three consonants in a row. *Each consonant is pronounced.*

Example: S K I N
(sk is a consonant blend.)

BEGINNING CONSONANT BLENDS

bl	–	blot	**pr**	–	press
br	–	brim	**sc**	–	scat
cl	–	clap	**sk**	–	skin
cr	–	crib	**sl**	–	sled
dr	–	drop	**sm**	–	smell
dw	–	dwell	**sn**	–	snap
fl	–	flag	**sp**	–	spot
fr	–	frizz	**st**	–	stop
gl	–	glad	**sw**	–	swim
gr	–	grab	**tr**	–	trip
pl	–	plan	**tw**	–	twin

The consonant blends must be pronounced quickly so that they blend together, almost as one sound.

Read with the teacher.

Read these words with the class or teacher. Mark the vowels..

CCVC

blĕd	drip	flap	glut	twig
blot	drag	flax	glob	twin
brag	drug	flex	glum	trim
brig	drum	fled	clam	trip
brat	flip	cram	clip	trap
bran	flop	crab	clap	grab
brim	flit	crib	club	grin
drab	flat	glad	slap	grim
drop	flag	glib	slop	grub
stop	spot	swim	slip	smug
stab	spit	swam	slam	snug
step	spin	swum	slim	snag

CCVCe

blāze	froze	grade	smoke	state
blame	frame	grope	smile	stale
blade	trade	prize	snake	stake
broke	truce	pride	snipe	stove
brake	tribe	prime	spine	stone
brave	grape	scale	spike	close
brute	gripe	skate	spoke	clone

Read with the teacher.

Write 5 words by adding **cl**, **fl**, **sl**, **sn**, and **tr** to the closed syllable **ap**.

1. ___clap___   4. _____

2. _____   5. _____

3. _____

Write 8 words by adding **cl**, **dr**, **fl**, **gr**, **sk**, **sl**, **sn**, and **tr** to the closed syllable **ip**.

1. _____   5. _____

2. _____   6. _____

3. _____   7. _____

4. _____   8. _____

Write 3 words by adding **br**, **sm**, and **sp** to the syllable **oke**.

1. _____   3. _____

2. _____

Write 5 words by adding **cr**, **sk**, **pl**, **sl**, and **st** to the syllable **ate**.

1. _____   4. _____

2. _____   5. _____

3. _____

Pronounce these words with the class or teacher.

Write 4 words by adding **br**, **gl**, **sl**, and **sn** to the syllable **ide**.

1. _____   3. _____

2. _____   4. _____

Write 11 words by adding **cr**, **dr**, **fl**, **fr**, **pl**, **pr**, **sk**, **sl**, **sp**, **st**, and **tr** to the vowel **y**.

1. _____   7. _____

2. _____   8. _____

3. _____   9. _____

4. _____   10. _____

5. _____   11. _____

6. _____

Write 7 words by adding **cr**, **dr**, **fl**, **pl**, **pr**, **sl**, and **st** to the closed syllable **op**.

1. _____   5. _____

2. _____   6. _____

3. _____   7. _____

4. _____

Write 4 words by adding **dw**, **sm**, **sp**, and **sw** to the syllable **ell**.

1. _____   3. _____

2. _____   4. _____

Pronounce these words with the class or teacher.

Read with the teacher.

Pronounce these words with the class or teacher.

tab	lid	pot	pin
stab	slid	spot	spin
win	rag	rip	rum
twin	drag	grip	drum
can	kid	lass	lap
scan	skid	class	clap
lot	mug	led	kill
slot	smug	sled	skill
lab	top	nap	cat
slab	stop	snap	scat
lip	less	lot	pill
flip	bless	plot	spill
tub	rib	lop	lug
stub	crib	flop	plug

Circle 15 words, both across and down.

S	C	A	T	Z	F	R	Y	G
T	R	A	P	B	L	A	B	R
O	X	X	C	R	A	B	R	A
V	P	S	T	A	G	E	I	B
E	S	L	Y	G	L	A	D	R
S	W	I	M	T	R	Y	E	A
S	S	P	O	T	R	I	P	T

WORD LIST

blab	slip
brag	sly
brat	spot
bride	stage
crab	stove
flag	swim
fry	trap
glad	trip
grab	try
scat	

Read with the teacher.

MAVERICK: Study this sight word with the teacher.

```
two
```

Some words that begin with **tw** come from the Old English language. In Old English, **twā** meant *two* or *double*. The words below contain the meaning *two*.

Word	*Meaning in Old English*
twelve	10 and 2 left over (10 + 2)
twenty	2 tens (2 × 10)
twice	double
twin	two by two; double
twine	two strings twisted together
twist	"two" and "rope"
twig	divided in two (a small branch growing out of a tree)

The teacher will dictate words which have consonant blends and short vowel sounds. On the first line, write the word that is dictated. On the line next to it, write the word again, adding an **e**. Pronounce the new word you have written.

Example: _____plan_____ _____plane_____

1. _____ _____ 6. _____ _____

2. _____ _____ 7. _____ _____

3. _____ _____ 8. _____ _____

4. _____ _____ 9. _____ _____

5. _____ _____ 10. _____ _____

Read with the teacher.

Make compound words.

1. class + mate = _____

2. grape + vine = _____

3. side + swipe = _____

4. fire + place = _____

5. drug + store = _____

6. bob + sled = _____

Match each word in Column A with its definition in Column B. Write the letter of your answer on the line next to the number. The first one has been done for you.

	Column A		Column B
__i__	1. slop	a.	sniff
_____	2. snip	b.	pig
_____	3. grip	c.	fire
_____	4. fly	d.	fly fast; move fast
_____	5. flit	e.	live
_____	6. scat	f.	grin
_____	7. smell	g.	cut
_____	8. blaze	h.	baby bed
_____	9. crib	i.	to spill; garbage
_____	10. dwell	j.	grasp; tote bag
_____	11. drove	k.	nasty
_____	12. snide	l.	go away
_____	13. swine	m.	past tense of *drive*
_____	14. slid	n.	past tense of *slide*
_____	15. smile	o.	to move in the sky; go fast; an insect

Beginning Consonant Blends

Read with the teacher.

Fill in the blanks to complete each sentence. Use the words from the list.

1. The two men have the sk_____ to win the

    bobsl_____ race.

2. Glen sw_____ in the lake at sunrise.

3. The man at the mine had gr_____ on his face.

4. We dr_____ the van to the Grand Canyon.

5. My cl_____ will begin at nine.

6. Did the bl_____ dr_____ fit Gwen?

7. Tim sl_____ in to home pl_____ to

    sc_____ a run.

8. Bruce fell on the ice and br_____ his leg.

9. Dale met Brad at the cl_____ .

10. Eve lit the fire on the gr_____ .

WORD LIST
blue
broke
class
club
dress
drove
grill
grime
plate
score
skill
sled
slid
swim

Circle all the words that are the same as the one on the left.

1. **globe** globqlobegoldglobeglobglobegfobelobeglobeqlobe

2. **twin** twinetuintmintwintwinfwinwintwentwimtwinlwinin

3. **true** turetrutrueturetrnetructrutruetruetruetruetrue

Read with the teacher.

Pronounce these common three-letter beginning consonant blends.

scr – scrap

spl – split

spr – sprig

str – strap

Copy these words. Pronounce them with the class or teacher.

1. scrap _____
2. scrape _____
3. scram _____
4. scrub _____
5. split _____
6. splice _____
7. spry _____

8. spruce _____
9. strip _____
10. stripe _____
11. strike _____
12. stroke _____
13. stress _____
14. strum _____

WORD FOCUS

Do this exercise orally with the teacher.

clot	twinge	frame	scrod

(The teacher will begin with a Vowel Drill.)

Read with the teacher.

In each set, read the first syllable. Point to the vowel and say its letter name. Next, say the *sound* of the vowel and read the *syllable*. Then, read the other two syllables.

1.	lom	**3.**	kib	**5.**	wen	**7.**	lif	**9.**	wit
	blom		skib		dwen		glif		swit
	brom		slib		dren		grif		smit

2.	rux	**4.**	lav	**6.**	rut	**8.**	wog	**10.**	rep
	prux		clav		prut		twog		trep
	plux		crav		sprut		trog		strep

Listen, then circle the syllable that the teacher says.

1.	dreg	breg	preg	greg	**4.**	dran	fran	pran	tran
2.	clup	slup	glup	frup	**5.**	scruv	stuv	struv	swuv
3.	dwix	twix	swix	snix	**6.**	trob	brob	frob	prob

The teacher will dictate three syllables.

1. _____ **2.** _____ **3.** _____

Work with the teacher.

Read the following sentences and insert them in the grid. (Note that the heading "When?" has been added to the grid.)

1. Brad woke Cliff at sunrise.

2. A snake slid into the pit.

3. The bride broke her leg on the step.

4. Glen drove the van to the game.

5. We met the girl at the bus stop.

6. The lake froze in the fall.

SUBJECT	VERB	OBJECT		
Who? (or What?)	*Did?*	*What? (or Whom?)*	*Where?*	*When?*
Brad	woke	Cliff		at sunrise.
A snake	slid		into the pit.	

WORDS

_____   _____

_____   _____

_____   _____

_____   _____

_____   _____

_____   _____

_____   _____

_____   _____

WORD GROUPS

_____

_____

_____

_____

_____

SENTENCES

_____

_____

_____

_____

Ending Consonant Blends

Read with the teacher.

ENDING CONSONANT BLENDS

ct – act		**nd** – sand	
ft – gift		**nt** – tent	
lf – self		**nx** – jinx	
ld – weld		**pt** – kept	
lk – milk		**sk** – desk	
lp – help		**sp** – gasp	
lt – melt		**st** – nest	
mp – lamp		**xt** – next	

Copy these words. Pronounce them with the class or teacher.

1. and _____
2. end _____
3. limp _____
4. left _____
5. must _____
6. belt _____
7. fact _____

8. lynx _____
9. went _____
10. gulp _____
11. lisp _____
12. dusk _____
13. gulf _____
14. pond _____

Read with the teacher.

Read these words with the class or teacher. Notice that the vowels have the short sound. The syllables are closed: CVCC. Mark the vowels.

land	hunt	left	bulb
lend	hint	lift	bulk
ramp	list	silk	next
romp	last	sulk	nest
fast	fund	dump	rent
fist	fond	damp	rest
band	must	desk	tent
bend	mist	dusk	test
bond	mast	disk	text

Follow the directions.

1. Write the word **west**. _____

2. Change the *w* to *b*. _____

3. Change the *b* to *qu*. _____

4. Change the *qu* to *n*. _____

5. Change the *s* to *x*. _____

6. Change the *n* to *t*. _____

7. Change the *x* to *n*. _____

8. Change the *e* to *i*. _____

9. Change the *n* to *l*. _____

10. Change the first *t* to *qu*. _____

11. Change the *qu* to *w*. _____

12. Change the *i* to *e*. _____

13. Change the *l* to *n*. _____

14. Change the *n* to *s*. _____

Read with the teacher.

Circle 20 words, both across and down.

B	E	S	T	Q	U	I	L	T
A	F	I	D	E	S	K	A	E
N	S	L	X	X	X	X	M	S
D	Z	K	R	A	F	T	P	T
D	U	S	T	E	N	D	Z	L
A	A	N	T	G	I	F	T	I
M	J	U	S	T	A	N	D	F
P	W	E	S	T	R	U	S	T

WORD LIST

and	just
ant	lamp
band	lift
best	quilt
damp	raft
desk	rust
dust	silk
end	test
gift	west

Divide these compound words.

1. himself = _____ + _____

2. myself = _____ + _____

3. itself = _____ + _____

4. yourself = _____ + _____

5. flagpole = _____ + _____

6. campfire = _____ + _____

7. sideswipe = _____ + _____

8. landslide = _____ + _____

9. sandpile = _____ + _____

MAVERICK: Study this sight word with the teacher.

sign

Ending Consonant Blends

Read with the teacher.

Fill in each blank with the correct word.

1. The plane from France is due to _____ at nine.
   lend   left   land

2. If you are late, you must go to the _____ of the line.
   and   end   imp

3. Do you like to _____ in the sun?
   bask   sand   dusk

4. An _____ bit Steve on the leg.
   ask   apt   asp

5. Will you _____ me $10?
   fund   cent   lend

6. His cat is _____ of mint candy.
   fond   gulp   fund

7. He went inside at _____ .
   dusk   desk   disk

8. The huge red and blue _____ said STOREWIDE
   send   sent   sign
   SALE.

9. I must use some of my _____ money to buy a fan
   rant   rent   runt
   belt for the van.

10. You will have to drill a hole in the base of the _____
    lump   limp   lamp
    for the wire.

Read with the teacher.

Many words have BEGINNING *and* ENDING consonant blends. In the words below, put a circle around each blend. Place a mark (ˇ) over the vowel in each word to show that it is *short*.

Example: (b l) ĕ (n d)

t w i s t	g r a n d	g r u n t
c r a m p	b l u n t	c r i s p
d r a f t	b l a s t	s l e p t
b l o n d	s t a m p	d r i f t
s p e n t	p r i n t	s k u l k

Write the definition for each word listed below. Use the dictionary. Work with the teacher.

1. scant _____

2. grasp _____

3. swift _____

Circle the words that are the same as the one on the left.

1. **flint** ftintflntfilntflintintflflintflitfluntfliutflintfint

2. **brisk** brishbrietbrskbiskbriskriskbreskbriskbriskbriskbrisk

3. **squint** sqintsquintsquintsguintquintsquiutsqntsquinsquintint

Read with the teacher.

Pronounce these words with the class or teacher.

rust	raft	lump
trust	draft	plump
crust	craft	clump
imp	ant	asp
blimp	grant	clasp
skimp	slant	grasp
and	amp	end
stand	clamp	spend
brand	tramp	blend

The teacher will pronounce 12 words. Write the *letter* of the vowel in each word.

1. _____   5. _____   9. _____

2. _____   6. _____   10. _____

3. _____   7. _____   11. _____

4. _____   8. _____   12. _____

Read with the teacher.

Complete each word by putting a vowel in the blank.

1. b ___ l t

2. ___ n d

3. f ___ n d

4. w ___ n t

5. l ___ m p

6. n ___ x t

7. g ___ l f

8. d ___ s k

9. k ___ p t

10. l ___ s t

11. f ___ c t

12. g ___ f t

13. w ___ l d

14. m ___ s t

15. b ___ n d

16. s ___ l f

17. t r ___ s t

18. s p ___ n d

19. c l ___ m p

20. p r ___ n t

Fill in each blank with the correct letter.

s i g n

s i ___ n

___ i ___ n

s i ___ ___

s ___ ___ n

s ___ ___ ___

___ ___ ___ ___

Work with the teacher.

CROSSWORD PUZZLE: Fill in each blank to make words across and down.

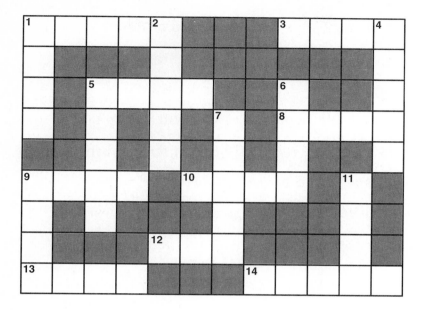

Across

1. Fast
3. Baby bed
5. Hit
8. Quiz
9. Not fat
10. Wet
12. Bug
13. Plot
14. Asp

Down

1. Cut
2. To walk on; hobo
4. Bad man
5. To take off; to rob
6. Come to a standstill; quit; rest; give up
7. Tilt
9. Spill
11. Take a chance

WORD LIST

ant	slop
brute	snake
crib	snip
damp	stop
plan	strip
risk	swift
slant	test
slap	tramp
slim	

Read with the teacher.

Read these word groups with the class or teacher. Circle all the words that contain consonant blends.

spend some time	a gulp of milk
a snake in the grass	must state your name
his smug smile	broke the bulb
and swam in the pond	will wilt in the sun
crust of the pie	a grin on his face
as snug as a bug in a rug	wore a red mask
rant and rave	quest in the west
will give a test	the blue sky at dusk
a fast raft	in a snug nest

Read these sentences with the class or teacher.

1. Next time I will cut the grass myself.
2. Do you plan to go by yourself?
3. The prince himself met me at the plane.
4. The cat hid itself in the crate.
5. I cut myself on the blade.
6. The baby cannot stand by himself yet.
7. Did the gate close by itself?
8. He is not himself since he left his job.
9. Do you hum to yourself?

WORD FOCUS

Do this exercise orally with the teacher.

vend	cyst	blond	sprint

(The teacher will begin with a Vowel Drill.)

Read with the teacher.

In each set, read the first syllable. Point to the vowel and say its letter name. Next, say the *sound* of the vowel and read the *syllable*. Then, read the following syllable or syllables.

1.	gom	3.	hul	5.	wen	7.	taf	9.	dis
	gomp		hulk		wend		taft		dist

2.	lex	4.	las	6.	rus	8.	pel	10.	cal
	lext		lasp		rust		pelt		calp
	plext		clasp		crust		spelt		scalp

Listen, then circle the syllable that the teacher says.

1.	dres	dresp	dreps	4.	rant	tran	trant
2.	nast	snat	sant	5.	skump	skum	skup
3.	wixt	twix	wix	6.	trost	tros	trots

The teacher will dictate three syllables.

1. _____   2. _____   3. _____

Work with the teacher.

Read the following sentences and insert them in the grid. (Note that "Can Do?" and "Will Do?" have been added under the VERB heading.)

1. Grace got a ride at ten.

2. The girl left a blueprint on my desk.

3. Stan will drive his bus to the lab.

4. We met the plane at five.

5. Brent broke his hand at the camp in June.

6. Sue will send a gift.

7. The cab made a dent in my van.

8. The men can get a job at the plant.

SUBJECT	VERB	OBJECT		
Who? (or What?)	*Did? Can do? Will do?*	*What? (or Whom?)*	*Where?*	*When?*

WORDS

_____   _____

_____   _____

_____   _____

_____   _____

_____   _____

_____   _____

_____   _____

WORD GROUPS

_____

_____

_____

_____

_____

SENTENCES

_____

_____

_____

_____

Word Families

Read with the teacher.

Words that end with consonant blends almost always contain *short* vowels. However, some words are exceptions to this rule.

The words below have *long* vowel sounds. The words in each box belong to a "word family." That is, they sound alike, or rhyme.

Pronounce these words with the class or teacher.

ōld	ōst	ōlt	īld	īnd
old	host	bolt	mild	bind
bold	most	colt	wild	blind
cold	post	jolt	child	find
fold	ghost	volt		grind
gold				kind
hold				mind
sold				rind
scold				wind*
told				

* <u>Wind</u> can be pronounced either / wĭnd / or / wīnd / with different meanings.

96

Read with the teacher.

Make compound words.

1. sign + post = _____

2. wild + life = _____

3. up + hold = _____

4. blind + fold = _____

5. post + man = _____

6. bill + fold = _____

7. wild + cat = _____

8. wind + up = _____

Read these word groups with the class or teacher. Circle all the words that belong to a "word family."

a wild old yak

hold in my mind

as pure as gold

and the ghost will flit

has sold the vest

the windup of the game

and told a lie

a bold brute

fold the dress

will save the wildlife

as cold as ice

on top of the signpost

Circle the words that are the same as the one on the left.

1. **mold** modlnoldwoldmolddmldmollmodlmuldmcldmoldwoldmold

2. **hind** himdhinhiudhinbhindhindhindhindhinhinbhnind

Read with the teacher.

Circle 22 words, both across and down.

```
G H O S T O Y F F X B I N D X M
O H H H O L D K I B L I N D S O
L H C O L D M I N D X Z B J C S
D M I L D W I N D P O S T X O T
C H I L D L L D B O L T C O L T
Y X Z W I L D F O L D S O L D B
```

WORD LIST	
bind	kind
blind	mild
bolt	mind
child	most
cold	old
colt	post
find	scold
fold	sold
ghost	told
gold	wild
hold	wind

Match each word in Column A with its definition in Column B. Write the letter of your answer on the line next to the number.

Column A	**Column B**
_____ 1. told	**a.** to grasp; to clasp; to grip
_____ 2. bind	**b.** past tense of *sell*
_____ 3. wild	**c.** to tie up; to tape up
_____ 4. sold	**d.** past tense of *tell*
_____ 5. hold	**e.** not tame
_____ 6. wind	**f.** to twist; to zigzag; to turn

Read these sentences with the class or teacher.

1. The old man told us the colt was sold.
2. The kind host did not scold the wild child.
3. Did the postman find the lost box of gold?
4. Two bold men swam in the ice-cold pond.
5. Close the gate and bolt it.
6. I will cut the rind from the lime, grind it up, and add it to the pie.

Read with the teacher.

Follow the directions.

1. Write the word **old**. _____

2. Add *c* to the beginning of **old**. _____

3. Change the *d* to *t*. _____

4. Change the *c* to *b*. _____

5. Change the *t* to *d*. _____

6. Change the *b* to *m*. _____

7. Change the *o* to *i*. _____

8. Change the *l* to *n*. _____

9. Change the *m* to *w*. _____

10. Change the *n* to *l*. _____

11. Change the *wi* to *go*. _____

12. Change the *g* to *h*. _____

13. Change the *h* to *f*. _____

14. Take away the *f*. _____

WORD FOCUS

Do this exercise orally with the teacher.

wind	host	scold	mild

(The teacher will begin with a Vowel Drill.)

Read with the teacher.

Read the "word family" syllables below. All vowel sounds are long. First, point to and say the three letters. Next, say the *long sound* of the vowel. Then, read the *syllable* and the word below it.

1. ind rind	**4.** old bold	**7.** ind blind	**10.** olt colt
2. olt volt	**5.** ild mild	**8.** olt bolt	**11.** old scold
3. ost post	**6.** ost host	**9.** old fold	**12.** ind grind

Listen, then circle the syllable that the teacher says.

1. spib	spab	speb	spob	**4.** quis	ques	quas	quos
2. fist	fest	fust	fast	**5.** tren	trin	trun	trin
3. dwim	dwum	dwom	dwem	**6.** hisk	hesk	hosk	hask

The teacher will dictate three syllables.

1. _____   **2.** _____   **3.** _____

SENTENCE FOCUS

Work with the teacher.

Read the first three sentences and insert them in the grid. Then, complete the next three sentences and insert them in the grid.

1. Bret sold his home by the lake last June.

2. Al can tame the wild colt.

3. I will drive the old man to the store at nine.

4. A postman left _____.

5. Gwen will find _____.

6. The child can hide _____.

SUBJECT	VERB	OBJECT		
Who? (or What?)	*Did? Can do? Will do?*	*What? (or Whom?)*	*Where?*	*When?*

WORDS

_____   _____

_____   _____

_____   _____

_____   _____

_____   _____

_____   _____

_____   _____

WORD GROUPS

_____

_____

_____

_____

_____

SENTENCES

_____

_____

_____

_____

More Sounds for the Letter a

A as in BALL

Read with the teacher.

The letter **a** usually sounds like / ȯ / when it has an **l** or **ll** after it. A dot over an **o** is the mark that most dictionaries use for this special sound.

Copy these words. Be prepared to pronounce them with the class or teacher.

1.	all	_____	**9.** wall	_____
2.	call	_____	**10.** squall	_____
3.	fall	_____	**11.** halt	_____
4.	hall	_____	**12.** malt	_____
5.	mall	_____	**13.** salt	_____
6.	small	_____	**14.** bald	_____
7.	tall	_____	**15.** scald	_____
8.	stall	_____	**16.** false	_____

MAVERICK: Study this sight word with the teacher.

what

Read with the teacher.

In the words **balk**, **talk**, **walk**, and **stalk**, the letter **l** is silent.

Write the pronunciation for the words below. Use the dictionary. The teacher will help you.

1. balk   bȯk _____

2. talk   _____

3. walk   _____

4. stalk   _____

The letter **a** in the words **water** and **want** can be pronounced two ways. Either is correct.

wȯter *or* wŏter

wȯnt *or* wŏnt

Read these sentences with the class or teacher.

1. The foreman will balk if his men go on strike.

2. What do you want? Do you want a tall glass of ice water or cold milk?

3. Do not walk on the damp grass.

4. Hot water will scald you if you spill it on yourself.

5. The stalk of the plant will dry up in the fall.

6. Did you see the girl at the mall? Did you talk to her?

Read with the teacher.

Make compound words.

1. water + fall = _____

2. side + walk = _____

3. dry + wall = _____

4. base + ball = _____

5. wind + fall = _____

6. cat + walk = _____

Fill in each blank with the correct word.

1. If you cannot go to the game, will you give me a _____ ?
    mall   calk   call

2. Ask Lance if he will tape the hole in the _____ .
    squall   balk   drywall

3. I just got a job on TV! What a _____ !
    waterfall   windfall   windbag

4. _____ do you want?
    what   want   walk

5. The huge tan tomcat had a big _____ spot on his left hip.
    balk   bald   scald

6. Walt met his wife at a drugstore in the _____ .
    mall   stall   tall

7. Jim is up on the _____ so he can fix an unsafe wire.
    sidewalk   catwalk   stalk

Read with the teacher.

An **antonym** is a word that means the opposite of another word. For example, the opposite of *hot* is *cold*.

The word **antonym** comes from the Greek language. **Ant-** means "the opposite of" and **-onym** means "name."

Draw a line from each word in the left column to the word in the right column with the <u>opposite</u> meaning.

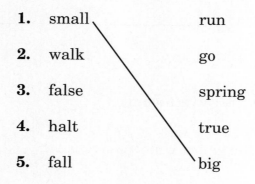

1. small	run
2. walk	go
3. false	spring
4. halt	true
5. fall	big

Circle 15 words, both across and down.

```
W  A  L  L  S  T  A  L  K
A  S  X  X  A  T  C  H  Z
L  S  M  A  L  T  A  A  B
K  C  A  A  T  A  L  L  A
A  A  L  S  T  A  L  L  L
L  L  L  B  A  L  L  Z  D
L  D  F  A  L  L  Z  K  K
```

WORD LIST

all	salt
bald	scald
ball	stalk
call	stall
fall	tall
hall	walk
mall	wall
malt	

Read with the teacher.

You can find the names of persons and places in the back section of most dictionaries. This section is called <u>Persons and Places</u> or <u>Biographical Names</u>. (In a few dictionaries, names and places are listed with all the other words.)

As a class assignment, answer the following questions and discuss **Dr. Jonas Salk**. Use the dictionary. Your teacher will help you.

1. Write the name of the section of your dictionary in which <u>Salk, Jonas,</u>

   is listed. _____

2. Write the <u>pronunciation</u> of his name. _____

3. When was he born? _____

4. In what country does he live? _____

5. Why is he famous? _____

   _____

REVIEW

So far, you have learned that the letter **a** can have these three sounds:

1. ă *as in* **at**
2. ā *as in* **safe**
3. ȯ *as in* **ball**

Read with the teacher.

When the letter **a** comes between a **w** and an **r**, it usually has the / ȯ / sound.

Copy these words.

1. war _____   4. warp _____

2. warm _____   5. ward _____

3. warn _____   6. wart _____

Pronounce these words with the class or teacher.

Follow the directions.

1. Write the word **war**. _____

2. Add *m* to the end of **war**. _____

3. Change *m* to *d*. _____

4. Change *d* to *n*. _____

5. Change *n* to *p*. _____

6. Change *p* to *t*. _____

7. Take away the *t*. _____

Read with the teacher.

Another sound for the letter **a** has two dots on top of the letter, like this: / ä /. It sounds like / ä / in the word **father**. This / ä / sound usually has an **r** after it, but not always.

Copy these words. MARK THE VOWELS WITH TWO DOTS. Pronounce the words with the class or teacher.

1. car _____

2. card _____

3. scar _____

4. scarf _____

5. arm _____

6. harm _____

7. hard _____

8. yard _____

9. yarn _____

10. jar _____

11. far _____

12. farm _____

13. bar _____

14. barn _____

15. bark _____

16. dark _____

17. mark _____

18. park _____

19. spark _____

20. art _____

21. cart _____

22. dart _____

23. part _____

24. smart _____

25. start _____

26. star _____

27. starve _____

28. carve _____

29. large _____

30. barge _____

Read with the teacher.

MAVERICK: Study this sight word with the teacher.

guard

Read these sentences with the class or teacher.

1. Marge and Art told us the test was hard.

2. The red barn was far from the farmyard.

3. A guard sat next to the gate of the space lab.

4. A barbell fell on Ward and broke his arm.

5. Nell left the jar of grape jam on the top of the stove.

6. The dark tan car drove by the park.

7. If you get some blue yarn, I will make a scarf for you.

8. The wet glass left a mark on the desk.

9. Your car will not run well if it has a bad spark plug.

10. Did you send a postcard to Mark?

11. Carl will give his child a ride in the cart.

12. Is Bart Garp a TV star?

Circle each word that contains the / ä / sound.

Read with the teacher.

Divide each compound word.

1. grandfather = _____ + _____

2. lifeguard = _____ + _____

3. barnyard = _____ + _____

4. landmark = _____ + _____

5. stargaze = _____ + _____

6. safeguard = _____ + _____

7. farmland = _____ + _____

8. wartime = _____ + _____

Fill in each blank with the correct letter.

guard

g ____ a r d

g ____ ____ r d

g ____ ____ r ____

____ ____ ____ r ____

____ ____ ____ ____ ____

what

w ____ a t

w h ____ t

w h ____ ____

____ h ____ ____

____ ____ ____ ____

Read with the teacher.

The letter **a** is also pronounced / ä / in these words:

calm   wad

palm   squad

swan   squat

swamp

Read these word groups with the class or teacher.

in the palm of my hand

did not call the squad car

a wad of gum

one swan in the blue water of the lake

a calm time at sunrise

and rose from the dark swamp

will squat by the warm campfire

Circle the words that are the same as the one on the left.

1. calm   camlalmoalmcalnclamcalcamlcalmcalmcalmcmalcalm

2. squad   sguadsqadsuadsquabsqadspuadsqabsqadsquadsqudsq

2. swan   suanswamswampswanpswanswamsansawnswswansnawans

WORD FOCUS

Do this exercise orally with the teacher.

| snarl | gall | balk | halt |

(The teacher will begin with a Vowel Drill.)

Read with the teacher.

Read each syllable as if it contains the vowel sound / ȯ /. First, point to and say the *name* of the vowel letter. Next, say the *sound* / ȯ /. Then, read the *syllable*.

1.	pall	**4.**	salse	**7.**	warb	**10.**	alt
2.	nald	**5.**	wald	**8.**	palt	**11.**	spald
3.	qual	**6.**	dwal	**9.**	snall	**12.**	dwalt

Listen, then circle the syllable that the teacher says. All syllables will contain the vowel sound / ä /, and the consonant sounds will vary.

1.	spar	sarp	spart	starp	**4.**	yarp	yark	yarb	yarg
2.	tarp	tarb	tarn	tarm	**5.**	blar	larb	blarb	bar!
3.	parm	darm	mard	pard	**6.**	hard	hart	harv	harf

The teacher will dictate three syllables.

1. _____   **2.** _____   **3.** _____

Work with the teacher.

Complete the following sentences and insert them in the grid.

1. _____ made a mark on the hall wall.

2. _____ can walk to the mall.

3. _____ will start in the park at nine.

4. _____ will call the guard next time.

5. _____ sold the farm.

6. _____ sat on the sidewalk.

SUBJECT	VERB	OBJECT		
Who? (or What?)	*Did? Can do? Will do?*	*What? (or Whom?)*	*Where?*	*When?*

DICTATION

WORDS

_____   _____

_____   _____

_____   _____

_____   _____

_____   _____

_____   _____

_____   _____

WORD GROUPS

_____

_____

_____

_____

_____

SENTENCES

_____

_____

_____

_____

Review

Read with the teacher.

Listen, then circle the word that the teacher says.

1.	hid	had	hide	hod
2.	sun	sign	sin	sane
3.	gem	gam	gym	gum
4.	get	gate	gut	got
5.	cam	came	calm	come
6.	rod	rid	red	rode
7.	slop	slap	slope	slip
8.	bake	broke	bark	brake
9.	must	most	mast	mist
10.	ball	bale	bill	bell
11.	gall	gull	gale	gill
12.	cede	side	sod	sad
13.	still	style	stale	stall
14.	mull	mule	mile	mill

Read with the teacher.

Fill in the blanks to complete the rule about the sound of the letter **c**.

> The letter **c** will sound like ____ if the
>
> letter ____ , ____ , or ____ comes after the **c**.

Read these words. If the **c** sounds like / s /, write **S** on the line. If the **c** sounds like / k /, write **K** on the line.

1. cast _____   4. talc _____   7. trance _____

2. cyst _____   5. cite _____   8. cede _____

3. crisp _____   6. ace _____   9. cove _____

Fill in the blanks to complete the rule about the sound of the letter **g**.

> The letter **g** will sound like ____ if the
>
> letter ____ , ____ , or ____ comes after the **g**.

Read these words. If the **g** sounds like / j /, write **J** on the line. If the **g** sounds like / g /, write **G** on the line.

1. sprig _____   4. large _____   7. gift _____

2. rage _____   5. get _____   8. gene _____

3. tinge _____   6. gem _____   9. gone _____

In two of the words above, the **g** does NOT follow the rule. Write those two words below.

_____   _____

Read with the teacher.

Read these sentences with the class or teacher. Then circle each word that contains a consonant blend.

1. Did the van sideswipe your cab?

2. The blond man in the red mask had a grin on his face.

3. Brice broke the bulb and cut himself.

4. The plant in the blue pot will wilt in the sun.

5. The gull made a snug nest on the top of the cliff.

6. A lynx is a small wildcat.

7. The crab dug a hole in the sand.

8. Twelve mice gave the old cat a fit.

Fill in the blanks to make each sentence complete. Use the words from the list.

1. S_____ from the b_____ made
   the s_____ dull and d_____ .

2. The l_____ on the d_____ had
   d_____ on it.

3. Tell Matt to t_____ the g_____
   n_____ to the wire fence.

4. A f_____ fell into my g_____ of
   m_____ . Yuk!

5. T_____ men swam in the race, but just
   t_____ made it to the w_____
   side of the huge lake.

WORD LIST
blaze
desk
drab
dust
fly
glass
grass
lamp
milk
next
sky
smoke
trim
twelve
two
west

Read with the teacher.

Pronounce these words with the class or teacher.

1.	lit	list	slit	7.	nip	snip	spin
2.	top	stop	spot	8.	fit	fist	fits
3.	bet	best	bets	9.	let	left	felt
4.	pan	span	snap	10.	sap	spat	past
5.	jut	juts	just	11.	kid	skid	disk
6.	rod	prod	drop	12.	lug	plug	gulp

Circle at least 20 words, both across and down.

```
C  A  M  P  R  P  A  S  T
A  A  P  I  T  A  F  A  T
T  F  P  E  S  T  M  O  R
F  I  S  T  E  E  G  P  A
A  T  E  N  T  E  N  T  M
S  I  F  T  G  R  U  T  R
T  I  J  U  T  A  U  M  A
R  A  T  G  A  S  P  S  F
P  A  N  T  O  J  U  S  T
```

WORD LIST	
camp	pest
cat	pit
fat	ram
fast	rat
fit	raft
fist	rut
gasp	set
jut	sift
just	ten
pat	tent
pant	tug
past	

REMINDER — So far, you have learned that the letter **a** can stand for these four sounds:

1. ă *as in* **at**

2. ā *as in* **safe**

3. ȯ *as in* **ball**

4. ä *as in* **father** *or* **car**

Read with the teacher.

The teacher will dictate 18 sight words.

1. _____   10. _____

2. _____   11. _____

3. _____   12. _____

4. _____   13. _____

5. _____   14. _____

6. _____   15. _____

7. _____   16. _____

8. _____   17. _____

9. _____   18. _____

Write the key words for each short vowel letter that the teacher says.

1. _____

2. _____

3. _____

4. _____

5. _____

What letter can be a vowel or a consonant? _____

Lesson 16

The Affix **ed**

Read with the teacher.

Words that show action are called *verbs*. The affix **ed** is added to the end of a verb to show that the action is "in the past." You can call **ed** the *past tense* affix.

Examples:	rent	+	ed	=	rented
	jump	+	ed	=	jumped
	call	+	ed	=	called

The **ed** affix makes three sounds:

1. / əd / as in **rented** sounds like / rĕntəd /.

   The word **rented** is a two-syllable word.* It has two vowel sounds. In the first syllable of **rented**, the letter **e** has a short sound. In the second syllable of **rented**, the **e** has a weaker sound. It sounds like a weak short **u**. This weak (or unstressed) sound is called the *schwa*. The symbol for the *schwa* sound looks like an upside-down **e**: / ə /.

   The *schwa* will be discussed again in Student Book 2.

2. / t / as in **jumped** sounds like / jumpt /.

3. / d / as in **called** sounds like / calld /.

---

* Remember, a syllable is a word or part of a word with one vowel sound.

Read with the teacher.

> If a word ends in **t** or **d**, the **ed** affix is a separate syllable. It is pronounced / əd /.

Do these exercises. Pronounce the words with the class or teacher.

1. add   + ed   =   ___added___
2. want + ed   =   _____
3. weld + ed   =   _____
4. end   + ed   =   _____
5. test + ed   =   _____
6. post + ed   =   _____
7. land + ed   =   _____
8. fold + ed   =   _____
9. hand + ed   =   _____
10. list + ed   =   _____
11. plant + ed   =   _____
12. start + ed   =   _____

Separate each root word from its affix.

1. _____rust_____ + __ed__ = rusted
2. _____ + _____ = funded
3. _____ + _____ = dusted
4. _____ + _____ = jolted
5. _____ + _____ = sanded
6. _____ + _____ = dented
7. _____ + _____ = blinded
8. _____ + _____ = trusted

Read with the teacher.

If words end in the voiceless* consonants
/ f /, / k /, / p /, / s /, / x /, / ch /, or / sh /,
the affix **ed** is pronounced / t /.

These words cannot be divided into syllables.

Do these exercises. Pronounce the words with the class or teacher.

1. stuff + ed = _stuffed_
2. talk + ed = _____
3. help + ed = _____
4. dress + ed = _____
5. fix + ed = _____
6. bark + ed = _____
7. pass + ed = _____
8. tax + ed = _____
9. ask + ed = _____
10. miss + ed = _____
11. dump + ed = _____
12. fuss + ed = _____
13. camp + ed = _____
14. staff + ed = _____

---

* A "voiceless" consonant is made with just a stream of breath — no sound is made in the voice box.

Read with the teacher.

> If words end in voiced sounds,
> the **ed** affix is pronounced / d /.
>
> These words cannot be divided into syllables.

Do these exercises. Pronounce the words with the class or teacher.

1. call + ed = _called_____
2. sign + ed = _____
3. film + ed = _____
4. buzz + ed = _____
5. warn + ed = _____
6. garb + ed = _____
7. yell + ed = _____
8. harm + ed = _____
9. fizz + ed = _____
10. snarl + ed = _____

Read these word groups with the class or teacher.

and handed us the bill

but the guard yelled at him

as the barge started to move

had wanted him to call

camped at a state park

warned the mob

if he signed his name

Read with the teacher.

First, write the two parts of each word. Then, write the letter or letters that show the sound of the **ed** affix.

If **ed** sounds like / əd /, write **əd** on the line.

If **ed** sounds like / t /, write **t** on the line.

If **ed** sounds like / d /, write **d** on the line.

əd? t? d?

1. _____part_____ + __ed__ = parted   __əd__
2. _____ + _____ = spilled   _____
3. _____ + _____ = lifted   _____
4. _____ + _____ = kissed   _____
5. _____ + _____ = blinded   _____
6. _____ + _____ = pinched   _____
7. _____ + _____ = killed   _____
8. _____ + _____ = fizzed   _____
9. _____ + _____ = scolded   _____
10. _____ + _____ = armed   _____
11. _____ + _____ = parked   _____
12. _____ + _____ = passed   _____
13. _____ + _____ = drifted   _____
14. _____ + _____ = twisted   _____

Read with the teacher.

First, pronounce the words in the Word List. Next, use the words to fill the blanks in the sentences below. Then, write each word in its correct place in the Crossword Puzzle on page 127.

Across

2. The dog _____ as a girl rode by on a bike.

4. Glen _____ the flat tire on his van.

8. The gas man _____ the stove and told us it was not safe.

9. The film _____ for a long time.

11. I drove into a signpost and _____ the grill on my car.

12. Don _____ his wife from Salt Lake City.

13. Mike _____ his grandfather move a desk into the den.

WORD LIST
asked
barked
blasted
called
dented
dressed
ended
fixed
folded
helped
lasted
melted
planted
rented
tested

Down

1. Joe _____ Jane for a date.

2. The spacecraft _____ off at sunrise.

3. We _____ a car for the trip upstate.

4. Gwen _____ the note and gave it to me.

5. The child was _____ in blue.

6. The class _____ at 9:30.

7. Brad _____ a grapevine next to the fence.

10. The ice _____ in the hot sun.

*The Affix **ed***

CROSSWORD PUZZLE: Use the words from page 126.

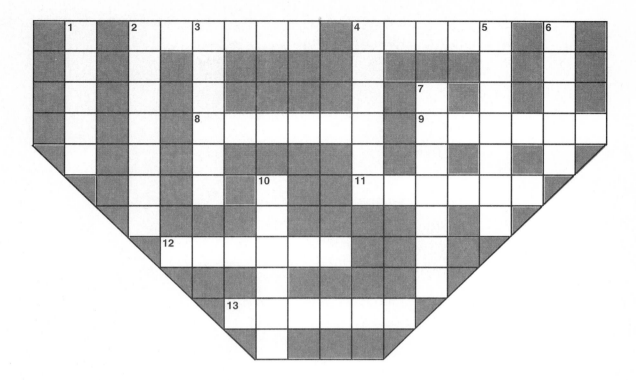

MAVERICK: Study this sight word with the teacher.

said

Fill in each blank with the correct letter.

said

s a __ d

s __ i d

s __ __ d

__ a __ d

s __ i __

__ __ i d

__ __ __ d

__ __ __ __

Read with the teacher.

Draw a line from each word in Column 1 to a word that means the same or almost the same in Column 2.

<u>**Column 1**</u>   <u>**Column 2**</u>

1. bumped   mended

2. fixed   walked

3. slanted   grasped

4. smelled   jolted

5. tramped   sniffed

6. clasped   tilted

IRREGULAR VERBS

Most words that take the affix **ed** are action words, called *verbs*. Some common verbs do not take the **ed** to form the past tense. They are irregular verbs.

Examples: *Present*   *Past*

   ride   rode (*not* rided)

   send   sent (*not* sended)

   hold   held (*not* holded)

WORD FOCUS

Do this exercise orally with the teacher.

bonded	filmed	talked

(The teacher will begin with a Vowel Drill.)

Read with the teacher.

Read these nonsense words with the class or teacher.

1.	glunted	**4.**	visted	**7.**	stanted	**10.**	flisked
2.	noxed	**5.**	honded	**8.**	prilmed	**11.**	snilled
3.	sarmed	**6.**	tisked	**9.**	clemped	**12.**	vinted

Listen, then circle the nonsense word that the teacher says.

1.	vusted	vosted	visted	**5.**	dimped	demped	domped
2.	nisked	nasked	nusked	**6.**	noxed	naxed	nuxed
3.	twilled	twelled	twulled	**7.**	silped	selped	sulped
4.	quixed	quaxed	quexed	**6.**	pelked	pilked	pulked

The teacher will dictate three syllables.

1. _____ 2. _____ 3. _____

SENTENCE FOCUS

Work with the teacher.

Read the first three sentences and insert them in the grid. Then, complete the next three sentences and insert them in the grid. (Note that the heading "Which?" has been added to the grid before the SUBJECT heading.)

1. The late film ended at two. (In this sentence, "The late" tells *which* film.)

2. A brave fireman scaled the wall. (In this sentence, "A brave" tells *which* fireman.)

3. The bald man walked his dog in the park.

4. _____ started a fire in the yard.

5. _____ camped at a lake last June.

6. _____ stuffed some trash in the can.

	SUBJECT	VERB	OBJECT		
Which?	*Who? (or What?)*	*Did? Can do? Will do?*	*What? (or Whom?)*	*Where?*	*When?*
The late	film	ended			at two.
A brave	fireman	scaled	the wall.		

130   *The Affix* **ed**

DICTATION

WORDS

_____   _____

_____   _____

_____   _____

_____   _____

_____   _____

_____   _____

_____   _____

WORD GROUPS

_____

_____

_____

_____

_____

SENTENCES

_____

_____

_____

_____

The Affix **ing**

Read with the teacher.

The affix **ing** is added to the end of a verb to mean "the act of doing."
You can call it the *doing* affix.

Examples: rest   +   ing   =   resting

Dave is *resting* on the bed.
What is Dave *doing*? (resting)

bark   +   ing   =   barking

The dog was *barking*.
What was the dog *doing*? (barking)

When the **ing** form means "doing," you must use a helping verb, such as:

is

am

are

was

were

Study the examples on the next page.

Read with the teacher.

Examples: The sun <u>is</u> <u>rising</u>.
I <u>am</u> <u>going</u> to the club.
The men <u>are</u> <u>lifting</u> the huge crate.
He <u>was</u> <u>walking</u> into the barn.
Steve and Mac <u>were</u> <u>yelling</u> at the soccer game.

Fill in each blank with the word at the left of the sentence. Add **ing** to each word.

1. sign   Vic is _____ his name at the top of the list.

2. fix   The two men were _____ the TV set.

3. be   Lynn said, "You are _____ rude!"

4. gulp   The child was _____ his milk.

5. send   I am _____ a get-well card to Pete.

6. weld   He is _____ the hole in the pipe.

7. wax   Bev and Tom are _____ the car.

8. hold   The fireman was _____ the hose.

9. park   Brad is _____ his car in a red zone.

Read with the teacher.

Join each root word and its affix. Then pronounce the words with the class or teacher.

1. sell + ing = _____

2. be   + ing = _____

3. hold + ing = _____

4. walk + ing = _____

5. rent + ing = _____

6. kiss + ing = _____

7. camp + ing = _____

8. spell + ing = _____

9. sign + ing = _____

10. warn + ing = _____

Circle 17 words, both across and down.

```
S P E L L I N G W A R N I N G T A L K I N G
E Y A A A Q R U A A B X N R E S T I N G G A
L G C S V N N L N A L R G S T U F F I N G D
L F H T S K D P T A S K I N G W D T V H O D
I H G I I I J I I S F F I X I N G I S M I I
N O D N B O N N N A C T I N G X X N G P N N
G S I G N I N G G G B E I N G J J G I N G G
```

WORD LIST

acting	going	resting	stuffing
adding	gulping	selling	talking
asking	lasting	signing	wanting
being	lifting	spelling	warning
fixing			

Read with the teacher.

Words with the **ing** affix can be used several ways in a sentence. Read the following sentences with the class or teacher. Notice how the **ing** forms are used.

1. <u>Parking</u> his car in a red zone, Brad ran into the store.

2. <u>Parking</u> in a red zone is not legal.

3. The <u>barking</u> dog ran after the car.

4. <u>Kissing</u> his wife, Matt ran up the steps into the plane.

5. The <u>spelling</u> test was hard.

6. We plan to go <u>camping</u> in June.

7. <u>Walking</u> in the park is a nice pastime.

8. The <u>warning</u> was posted on the wall.

Pronounce these words with the class or teacher.

falling	planting	acting
testing	being	buzzing
warning	lifting	asking
guarding	passing	jumping
holding	yelling	twisting
starting	adding	ending
drifting	farming	scolding
filling	missing	calling
going	finding	dusting

Read with the teacher.

Follow the directions.

1. Write the word **spelling**. _____
2. Change the *e* to *i*. _____
3. Change *sp* to *dr*. _____
4. Change *dr* to *k*. _____
5. Change the *k* to *w*. _____
6. Change the *w* to *t*. _____
7. Change the *i* to *e*. _____
8. Change the *t* to *y*. _____
9. Change the *y* to *dw*. _____
10. Change the *d* to *s*. _____
11. Change the *w* to *m*. _____
12. Take away the *m*. _____
13. Add *p* after the *s*. _____

Circle all the words that are the same as the one on the left.

1. **welding** weldingwellingwelbingweldnigweldignweldingwalding

2. **pressing** perssingpresingpessingperssignpressingpresingprng

3. **farming** framingfromingfamingfarmignfarmnigfarmngfarmingng

4. **jolting** joltngjotlingjoltinggoltingioltingjoltingjoltingn

WORD FOCUS

Do this exercise orally with the teacher.

sulking	grasping

SENTENCE FOCUS

Work with the teacher.

Complete the sentences in the grid. Then, write the sentences on the lines below the grid. The first one has been done for you. (Note that "Doing?" has been added under the VERB heading.)

	SUBJECT	VERB	OBJECT		
Which?	*Who? (or What?)*	*Doing?*	*What? (or Whom?)*	*Where?*	*When?*
The tall	man	is fixing	the sink.		
		was resting			
		are lifting			
		was selling			

1. <u>The tall man is fixing the sink.</u>

2. _____

3. _____

4. _____

WORDS

_____   _____

_____   _____

_____   _____

_____   _____

_____   _____

_____   _____

_____   _____

WORD GROUPS

_____

_____

_____

_____

_____

SENTENCES

_____

_____

_____

_____

The Silent **e** Spelling Rule

If a word ends with a silent **e**, drop the **e**
before adding an affix that starts with a vowel.

Example: hope   +   ing   =   hoping

The first letter of *ing* is a vowel, so
the **e** is dropped from the root word **hope**.

Study these examples:

make + ing = making
rise + ing = rising

Remember, the affix **ed** means "in the past." When you add **ed** to a word
that ends with a silent **e**, drop the **e** in the root word. You must add the
whole affix. Do not add **d** alone because **d** by itself has no meaning.

Examples: hope + ed = hoped
rule + ed = ruled
like + ed = liked

139

Read with the teacher.

Join each root and its affix. Remember to drop the silent **e** from the root word.

1. bake + ing = <u>baking</u>

2. vote + ed = _____

3. dine + ing = _____

4. smoke + ed = _____

5. hate + ed = _____

6. love + ing = _____

7. ice + ing = _____

8. hope + ed = _____

9. rise + ing = _____

10. strike + ing = _____

11. glue + ed = _____

12. poke + ed = _____

13. tube + ing = _____

14. style + ed = _____

15. pile + ing = _____

16. face + ed = _____

17. lie + ed = _____

18. flame + ing = _____

19. slope + ed = _____

20. like + ed = _____

21. rage + ing = _____

22. hide + ing = _____

Work with the teacher.

Do the following exercise.

1. The root word of **used** is ___use___ .

2. The root word of **named** is _____ .

3. The root word of **taking** is _____ .

4. The root word of **hoped** is _____ .

5. The root word of **smiling** is _____ .

6. The root word of **taped** is _____ .

7. The root word of **filling** is _____ .

8. The root word of **filing** is _____ .

9. The root word of **stored** is _____ .

10. The root word of **baking** is _____ .

Join each root and its affix. Remember to drop the silent **e** from the root word.

1. blaze + ing = ___blazing___

2. blaze + ed = _____

3. use + ing = _____

4. bite + ing = _____

5. place + ed = _____

6. smoke + ing = _____

7. tie + ed = _____

8. note + ing = _____

9. close + ed = _____

10. tape + ed = _____

11. smile + ed = _____

12. store + ing = _____

Read with the teacher.

Separate each root word from its affix.

1. _____tape_____ + ___ed___ = taped
2. _____ + _____ = filled
3. _____ + _____ = filed
4. _____ + _____ = using
5. _____ + _____ = smiling
6. _____ + _____ = stored
7. _____ + _____ = going
8. _____ + _____ = folded
9. _____ + _____ = tied
10. _____ + _____ = joking
11. _____ + _____ = sliding
12. _____ + _____ = priced
13. _____ + _____ = baking
14. _____ + _____ = taking
15. _____ + _____ = hiked

Draw a line from each word in the left column to a word that means the <u>opposite</u> in the right column.

1. taking   falling
2. riding   hated
3. loved   fired
4. saving   giving
5. rising   walking
6. hired   spending

    The Silent e Spelling Rule

Read with the teacher.

In Lesson 16, you learned that the affix **ed** can make three sounds.

First, write the parts of each word. Then write the letter that shows the sound of the **ed** affix.

əd? t? d?

1. _____use_____ + _ed_ = used _____d_____

2. _____joke_____ + _ed_ = joked _____t_____

3. _____ + _____ = ruled _____

4. _____ + _____ = named _____

5. _____ + _____ = traded _____

6. _____ + _____ = iced _____

7. _____ + _____ = skated _____

Each sentence contains a word that is not correct. First, circle the incorrect word. Then, write the correct word on the line at the end of the sentence.

1. Fran is (marking) a dress for the dance. _____making_____

2. The man walled home from the bus stop. _____

3. Greg was hiked for the job. _____

4. My wife barked a cake for the party. _____

5. Rob is talking his car in for a tune-up. _____

6. The lifeguard sated the life of the girl. _____

Read with the teacher.

Add **ed** to as many of these words as possible. Be careful! The affix **ed** cannot be used with some of the words. Add **ing** to the words that cannot take **ed**.

Pronounce the words with the class or teacher.

1. love + _ed_ = _loved_
2. rise + _____ = _____
3. save + _____ = _____
4. make + _____ = _____
5. drive + _____ = _____
6. blame + _____ = _____
7. gripe + _____ = _____
8. grope + _____ = _____
9. give + _____ = _____
10. bite + _____ = _____
11. take + _____ = _____
12. dine + _____ = _____
13. grade + _____ = _____
14. slide + _____ = _____
15. hate + _____ = _____
16. ride + _____ = _____
17. rake + _____ = _____
18. swipe + _____ = _____
19. date + _____ = _____
20. tune + _____ = _____

THE AFFIX Y

The letter **y** at the end of a word can be an affix. If the **y** is used as an affix, it can mean "having," "full of," "inclined to," or "small."

Remember that **y** is a vowel at the end of a word. You will drop the silent **e** in the root word before adding the affix **y**.

Example: rose   +   y   =   rosy

Do this exercise.

1. babe   + y   =   _baby_

2. craze   + y   =   _____

3. smoke + y   =   _____

4. nose   + y   =   _____

5. ice   + y   =   _____

6. lace   + y   =   _____

7. grime + y   =   _____

8. haze   + y   =   _____

Circle each word that is the same as the one on the left.

1. nosy   noseynosenosynozyuosynosynoseynosenosynosnosey

2. smoky smukysmokeysmockysmokysmokesmoksmokeysmokvsmok

3. slimy slimmyslimeyslimeslimeyslimyslimyslimyslimyimy

Read these words with the class or teacher.

1. rose   rosy
2. ice   icy
3. bite   biting
4. take   taking
5. ride   riding
6. drive   driving
7. like   liked   liking
8. dance   danced   dancing
9. skate   skated   skating
10. poke   poked   poking
11. trade   traded   trading
12. type   typed   typing
13. dine   dined   dining
14. gripe   griped   griping
15. grope   groped   groping
16. save   saved   saving
17. fence   fenced   fencing
18. bone   bony   boned   boning
19. smoke   smoky   smoked   smoking
20. ice   icy   iced   icing

REVIEW

If a word ends with a _____ _____ , drop the ____ before adding an affix that starts with a _____ .

WORD FOCUS

Do this exercise orally with the teacher.

| voted | slicing | closed | typing |

Work with the teacher.

Read the first three sentences below and insert them in the grid. Then complete the next three sentences and insert them in the grid. (Note that "Whose?" and "How Many?" have been added to the first heading.)

1. His wife is taking the cat to the vet.

2. The tall, slim girl skated on the pond at sunset.

3. Two old men were poking in the fireplace.

4. _____ was biting _____ .

5. _____ hiked _____ .

6. _____ is driving _____ .

	SUBJECT	VERB	OBJECT		
Which? Whose? How Many?	**Who? (or What?)**	**Did? Doing? Can do? Will do?**	**What? (or Whom?)**	**Where?**	**When?**
His	wife	is taking	the cat	to the vet.	

WORDS

_____   _____

_____   _____

_____   _____

_____   _____

_____   _____

_____   _____

_____   _____

WORD GROUPS

_____

_____

_____

_____

_____

SENTENCES

_____

_____

_____

_____

More Sounds for the Letters **o** and **u**

O as in DOG

Read with the teacher.

In some words, the letter **o** is pronounced / ȯ /. However, the pronunciation of this vowel may be different in various parts of the country. Dictionaries may show three sounds: / ȯ /, / ô /, and / ŏ /. In this book, the dot will be used: / ȯ /.

Read these words with the class or teacher.

bog	jog	boss	cost
clog	log	cross	lost
fog	eggnog	gloss	frost
frog	off	loss	soft
hog	scoff	toss	golf

MAVERICK: Study this sight word with the teacher.

often

Read with the teacher.

Fill in each blank with the correct letter.

often

o f __ e n

o f __ __ n

__ f t __ n

o f __ e __

o __ __ e __

__ __ __ e __

__ __ __ __ __

Each sentence contains a word that is not correct. First, circle the incorrect word. Then write the correct word on the line at the end of the sentence.

1. Ross and Mac often (jig) in the park. _jog_____

2. The fog jumped into the pond. _____

3. My pen fell of the desk. _____

4. The old bog barked at a car passing by. _____

5. Kyle loss his bus pass at the mall. _____

6. A dense log drifted in from the west. _____

7. I made some egghog for the party. _____

8. Liz lost a gulf ball in the pond. _____

Read with the teacher.

CROSSWORD PUZZLE: First, pronounce the words in the word list. Use the words to fill in the blanks in the sentences. Then write each word in its correct place in the crossword puzzle.

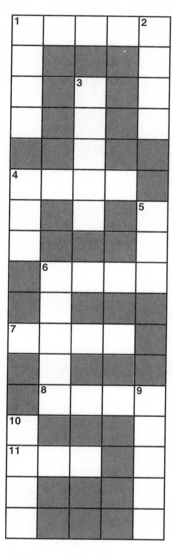

WORD LIST

boss	frost
cost	gloss
frog	fog
loss	log
lost	off
soft	scoff
cross	toss

Across

1. "You must use the _____ walk," said the cop to the child.

4. Mark _____ his billfold on the bus.

6. The _____ jumped into the pond.

7. My _____ got mad at me for being late.

8. The man yelled, " _____ the golf ball to me!"

11. The plane will take _____ at 7:45 AM sharp.

Down

1. His car _____ $8,000.

2. My waterbed felt so warm and _____ !

3. The brass lamp lost its shiny _____ .

4. Joe tossed a huge _____ into the fireplace.

5. I often have to drive in a dense _____ .

6. "Do you want me to _____ the cake?" Meg asked.

9. The girl said, "It was rude of you to _____ at me."

10. The _____ of his billfold upset Mark.

Follow the directions.

1. Write the word **fog**. _____

2. Change the *f* to *h*. _____

3. Change the *h* to *b*. _____

4. Change the *g* to *ss*. _____

5. Change the *b* to *t*. _____

6. Change the *t* to *cr*. _____

7. Change the *cr* to *gl*. _____

8. Take away the *g*. _____

9. Change the *ss* to *g*. _____

10. Change the *g* to *st*. _____

11. Change the *l* to *c*. _____

12. Change the *c* to *fr*. _____

13. Change the *st* to *g*. _____

14. Take away the *r*. _____

Join each root word and its affix.

1. scoff + ed = _____

2. frost + y = _____

3. golf + ing = _____

4. boss + y = _____

5. cross + ed = _____

6. toss + ing = _____

7. gloss + y = _____

8. cost + ing = _____

Read with the teacher

Only a few words contain the vowel **u** that sounds like / ŏŏ /. These are the most common:

put	push
full	bush
bull	pudding
pull	bulldog

Fill in each blank with a word from the list above.

1. A wild _____ broke the fence and bolted into the farmyard.

2. The sky was _____ of smoke from the fire.

3. Marty _____ an egg on the plate next to the ham.

4. Do you like rice _____ ?

5. The red fox was hiding behind a _____ by the side of the barn.

6. If you _____ and I _____ , we can move the old rusty gate.

7. Will your _____ bite me if I try to pet him?

REVIEW

So far, you have learned four sounds for the letter **u** and three sounds for the letter **o**:

Sounds for the letter u	Sounds for the letter o
1. ŭ *as in* **up**	1. ŏ *as in* **ox**
2. ū *as in* **mule**	2. ō *as in* **vote**
3. ōō *as in* **rule**	3. ȯ *as in* **dog**
4. ŏŏ *as in* **put**	

Read with the teacher.

Write an antonym for each word. Choose a word from the Word List.

1. The opposite of **pull** is _____ .

2. The opposite of **on** is _____ .

3. The opposite of **walk** is _____ .

4. The opposite of **hard** is _____ .

5. The opposite of **dull** is _____ .

WORD LIST

glossy
jog
off
push
soft

Circle at least 22 words, both across and down.

```
P U S H J O G P U T C L O G
F F S O J T P U X C T O S S
F R O G S M U D C F R C G N
E O O B U L L D O G B O G B
G S G S O X L I S L J S S U
G T P C T S Y N T O C R S S
N L L O S T S G M S O F T H
O F F F U L L L O S S B O T
G O L F L L O G G O F T E N
```

WORD LIST

bog	jog
bull	log
bush	loss
clog	lost
cost	off
dog	often
eggnog	pudding
frog	pull
frost	push
full	put
gloss	scoff
golf	soft
hog	toss

WORD FOCUS

Do this exercise orally with the teacher.

flossed	pulling

Work with the teacher.

Complete four sentences in the grid. Then write the sentences on the lines below the grid.

| Which? Whose? How many? | SUBJECT | VERB | OBJECT | | |
	Who? (or What?)	Did? Doing? Can do? Will do?	What? (or Whom?)	Where?	When?
My	boss	put			
		tossed	the baseball		
	ox	will pull			
The lost	bulldog				

1. _____

2. _____

3. _____

4. _____

DICTATION

WORDS

_____   _____

_____   _____

_____   _____

_____   _____

_____   _____

_____   _____

WORD GROUPS

_____

_____

_____

_____

_____

SENTENCES

_____

_____

_____

_____

Alphabetizing

Write the alphabet on the line below.

_____

Read with the teacher.

Put each group of letters in alphabetical order.

Example: l m o n   <u>l m n o</u>

1. b d c a   _____

2. h j k i   _____

3. r s p q   _____

4. b e d c   _____

5. x z w y   _____

6. i h g f   _____

7. h r e b   _____

8. s x t o   _____

9. n q d j   _____

10. m z k g   _____

11. w f u c   _____

12. l d v p   _____

Read with the teacher.

Look at each word at the left. Where would you find these words in the dictionary? Circle the correct answer.

1. **lark**   near the beginning   (near the middle)   near the end

2. **yard**   near the beginning   near the middle   near the end

3. **next**   near the beginning   near the middle   near the end

4. **bond**   near the beginning   near the middle   near the end

5. **scald**   near the beginning   near the middle   near the end

6. **dust**   near the beginning   near the middle   near the end

7. **use**   near the beginning   near the middle   near the end

8. **kind**   near the beginning   near the middle   near the end

Look at the words in each line. On the blank, write the word that comes *first* in alphabetical order.

1. fall   hall   call   _call_

2. host   most   ghost   _____

3. west   vest   test   _____

4. rag   rage   rake   _____

5. prime   quite   quit   _____

6. war   warn   warm   _____

7. quart   guard   post   _____

8. jam   ice   kid   _____

Work with the teacher.

Put these words in alphabetical order.

Example: scat   _art_

pet   _gold_

art   _pet_

gold   _scat_

1. mud   _____

hat   _____

web   _____

bid   _____

4. kite   _____

yard   _____

cast   _____

lax   _____

2. sob   _____

kid   _____

tub   _____

fin   _____

5. gas   _____

fate   _____

joke   _____

hill   _____

3. pit   _____

ant   _____

bug   _____

man   _____

6. grass   _____

rust   _____

dump   _____

sky   _____

Put these words in alphabetical order.

7. skid _____

spot _____

snip _____

stab _____

8. dust _____

drab _____

damp _____

desk _____

9. lamp _____

left _____

lost _____

lift _____

10. ask _____

ant _____

ace _____

ate _____

11. blaze _____

bump _____

bite _____

bold _____

12. gag _____

gym _____

gin _____

get _____

13. gasp _____

grab _____

glad _____

girl _____

14. mask _____

miss _____

must _____

mess _____

Put these words in alphabetical order.

15. wild   _____

      wind   _____

      wise   _____

      wire   _____

19. brave   _____

      brace   _____

      brake   _____

      brand   _____

16. stop   _____

      stun   _____

      stand   _____

      step   _____

20. flag   _____

      flat   _____

      flab   _____

      flap   _____

17. yap   _____

      yak   _____

      yard   _____

      yam   _____

21. quit   _____

      quill   _____

      quip   _____

      quiz   _____

18. glad   _____

      globe   _____

      glide   _____

      glum   _____

22. trace   _____

      trade   _____

      tramp   _____

      trap   _____

Read with the teacher.

Below at the left is a list of names. Put each name in the correct column.

	FEMALES	MALES

Kate
Liz
Tom
Bruce
Jeff
Pam
Jill
Tim
Dan
Mike
Jane
Fran
Jan
Don
Eve
Brad

FEMALES
_____
_____
_____
_____
_____
_____
_____

MALES
_____
_____
_____
_____
_____
_____
_____

Put the names in alphabetical order in the correct column.

MALES
_____
_____
_____
_____
_____
_____
_____

FEMALES
_____
_____
_____
_____
_____
_____
_____

Read with the teacher.

Below are names from a telephone directory. Put the names in alphabetical order. The teacher will help you.

1. Kent, Lyle W.   <u>Cole, Brent T.</u>

    Gage, Marge   _____

    Nelson, Bruce   _____

    Cole, Brent T.   _____

    Olds, J. C.   _____

    Nye, Glen & Jill   _____

2. Bell, Lynn   _____

    Bell, S.   _____

    Bell, Karl   _____

    Bell, Max   _____

    Bell, Scott   _____

    Bell, S. K.   _____

3. Dix, Randy   _____

    Danson, A. R.   _____

    Degman, Rose Ann   _____

    Dobbs, Gale   _____

    Degman, Ross C.   _____

    Dagg, Jan   _____

Read with the teacher.

These are some of the *sight words* you have studied. In Column 1, copy the words. In Column 2, put the words in alphabetical order.

Mavericks	*Column 1*	*Column 2*
1. of	_____	_____
2. are	_____	_____
3. was	_____	_____
4. were	_____	_____
5. you	_____	_____
6. here	_____	_____
7. from	_____	_____
8. eye	_____	_____
9. sign	_____	_____
10. often	_____	_____
11. guard	_____	_____
12. said	_____	_____

Work with the teacher.

The words in each group below are arranged in alphabetical order. But they make no sense! Try to unscramble the words in each group so that they form correct sentences.

1. due is My rent.

   _____

2. dog has lice Your.

   _____

3. guard gun his pulled The.

   _____

4. bag blue in money Put the the.

   _____

Review

Read with the teacher.

Match each word in Column A with a word that means the *same* in Column B. Write the letter of your answer on the line next to the number.

	Column A		Column B
_g_	1. crib	a.	mad
___	2. pig	b.	mist
___	3. ate	c.	large
___	4. stop	d.	icy
___	5. jog	e.	dined
___	6. fog	f.	hog
___	7. trade	g.	bed
___	8. frosty	h.	trot
___	9. huge	i.	swap
___	10. crazy	j.	halt
___	11. cap	k.	snip
___	12. cut	l.	hat

Work with the teacher.

Join each root word and its affix.

1. make + ing = <u>making</u>

2. smile + ed = _____

3. risk + y = _____

4. file + ing = _____

5. fill + ing = _____

6. name + ed = _____

7. joke + ing = _____

8. nose + y = _____

9. farm + ed = _____

10. cure + ing = _____

11. pump + ed = _____

12. boss + y = _____

13. wake + ing = _____

14. use + ed = _____

15. hide + ing = _____

16. wipe + ed = _____

17. hunt + ed = _____

18. grime + y = _____

19. gaze + ing = _____

20. smoke + y = _____

Work with the teacher.

Do this exercise.

1. The root word of **rosy** is _____rose_____

2. The root word of **pulling** is _____

3. The root word of **using** is _____

4. The root word of **wired** is _____

5. The root word of **bony** is _____

6. The root word of **faced** is _____

7. The root word of **cured** is _____

8. The root word of **piling** is _____

9. The root word of **hating** is _____

10. The root word of **grimy** is _____

11. The root word of **poked** is _____

12. The root word of **waved** is _____

13. The root word of **filling** is _____

14. The root word of **filing** is _____

15. The root word of **baby** is _____

Separate each root word from its affix.

1. _____bake_____ + _____ed_____ = baked

2. _____ + _____ = filing

3. _____ + _____ = slimy

4. _____ + _____ = quoting

5. _____ + _____ = paved

Read with the teacher.

Circle 25 words, both across and down.

```
F  A  C  I  N  G  F  S
A  R  A  C  E  D  A  A
D  T  T  Y  P  I  N  G
E  F  A  N  C  Y  O  I
D  I  N  E  R  O  F  F
I  L  A  C  Y  X  T  T
N  E  F  E  N  C  E  D
I  T  R  A  C  I  N  G
N  O  S  K  A  T  E  Y
G  S  M  O  K  Y  T  M
```

WORD LIST

art	icy
city	lacy
cry	net
dine	no
dining	off
facing	often
faded	raced
fan	sag
fancy	skate
fenced	smoky
file	tracing
gift	typing
gym	

An *antonym* is a word that means the opposite of another word. Match each word in Column A with a word that means the *opposite* in Column B. Write the letter of your answer on the line next to the number.

	Column A		Column B
_____	1. love	a.	dry
_____	2. save	b.	drop
_____	3. city	c.	fall
_____	4. you	d.	me
_____	5. came	e.	went
_____	6. wet	f.	hate
_____	7. rise	g.	farm
_____	8. lift	h.	spend

Read with the teacher.

Listen, then circle the word that the teacher says.

1. bell   ball   bull   bill
2. cud   cod   cad   code
3. ride   rode   rid   rude
4. den   din   done   dine
5. list   lust   lost   last
6. pill   pile   pull   pale
7. mast   must   most   mist
8. taping   tapping   tipping   typing
9. slat   slot   slate   slit
10. doll   dull   dill   dell
11. sad   said   side   sod
12. slime   slim   slam   slum
13. missed   messed   mussed   massed
14. stole   still   style   stale
15. fist   fussed   faced   fast
16. scat   skate   Scot   skit
17. kissed   cast   cost   cyst
18. bass   base   boss   bus
19. jug   jog   jag   jig
20. scaled   scald   scold   skilled

Work with the teacher.

Put these names in alphabetical order.

1. Bond, Mark W.   Benson, Van D.

2. Cosby, Dale   _____

3. Brant, V. R.   _____

4. Benson, Van D.   _____

5. Mott, G. L.   _____

6. Kane, Dan   _____

1. Wells, Greg   _____

2. Cobb, Brice T.   _____

3. Watson, G. S.   _____

4. Kerr, Brent   _____

5. Karr, Rex   _____

6. Mason, Les   _____

1. Webb, T. W.   _____

2. Rand, Jill   _____

3. Webb, Pat   _____

4. Carbin, Ted   _____

5. Danson, Glen M.   _____

6. Rand, Gale   _____

Read with the teacher.

Review the vowel sounds that you have learned so far. Read the word lists below.

Sounds of the letter **a**

ă *as in* **at**	ā *as in* **safe**	ȯ *as in* **ball**	ä *as in* **father, car**
1. fast	1. wave	1. talk	1. smart
2. grab	2. graze	2. bald	2. palm
3. stamp	3. snake	3. halt	3. hard

Sounds of the letter **e**

ĕ *as in* **Ed**	ē *as in* **eve, me, see**
1. bell	1. Gene
2. desk	2. we
3. trend	3. fee

Sounds of the letter **i**

ĭ *as in* **if**	ī *as in* **dime, tie**
1. twin	1. rice
2. list	2. lie
3. cliff	3. gripe

Sounds of the letter **o**

ŏ *as in* **ox**	ō *as in* **vote, toe**	ȯ *as in* **dog**
1. snob	1. grove	1. boss
2. clot	2. foe	2. golf
3. blond	3. smoke	3. lost

Sounds of the letter **u**

ŭ *as in* **up**	ū *as in* **mule**	o͞o *as in* **rule, sue**	o͝o *as in* **put**
1. stun	1. fuse	1. rude	1. bull
2. trust	2. mute	2. blue	2. pull
3. plump	3. fume	3. brute	3. full

Sounds of the letter **y**

ĭ *as in* **gym**	ī *as in* **type, by**	ē *as in* **happy**
1. gyp	1. tyke	1. baby
2. cyst	2. my	2. navy

Read with the teacher.

Complete each word by putting a vowel in the blank.

1. ___ ff

2. p ___ lling

3. f ___ nce

4. f ___ lded

5. b ___ rking

6. g ___ ft

7. t ___ pe

8. r ___ nted

9. f ___ lmed

10. fr ___ st

11. st ___ mp

12. b ___ ss

The teacher will dictate 20 sight words.

1. _____

2. _____

3. _____

4. _____

5. _____

6. _____

7. _____

8. _____

9. _____

10. _____

11. _____

12. _____

13. _____

14. _____

15. _____

16. _____

17. _____

18. _____

19. _____

20. _____

Name _____

Read the directions with the teacher.

A.

1. Write the alphabet. _____

_____ *(26 points)*

2. Write the vowel letters. _____ *(5 points)*

3. What letter can be a vowel or a consonant? _____ *(1 point)*

B.

One word in each row is a SIGHT WORD. Circle it. *(2 points)*

1. pill   rot   of   fun
2. safe   have   pie   robe

C.

Write **L** if the vowel within the word is LONG. Write **S** if the vowel is SHORT. *(10 points)*

Example: hat ___S___   dime ___L___

1.	tap _____	6.	wine _____
2.	tape _____	7.	mess _____
3.	rod _____	8.	robe _____
4.	fizz _____	9.	tune _____
5.	hum _____	10.	pet _____

D.

Listen, then circle the word that the teacher says. *(6 points)*

1. hat   hot   hit   hut
2. rod   rode   rude   rid
3. mule   mile   mole   male
4. pin   pane   pan   pine
5. nut   net   note   not
6. dome   dime   dim   dame

Name _____

Read the directions with the teacher.

A.

Fill in the blanks to complete the rule about the sound of the letter **c**.
(3 points)

> The letter **c** will sound like / s / if the
>
> letter ____ , ____ , or ____ comes after the **c**.

B.

Write **S** if the **c** letter sounds like / s /. Write **K** if the **c** letter sounds like / k /. *(6 points)*

Example: cot ___K___   city ___S___

1. cape _____   4. cove _____

2. cite _____   5. ice _____

3. cub _____   6. cell _____

C.

Write **S** if the **s** letter sounds like / s /. Write **Z** if the **z** letter sounds like / z /. *(6 points)*

Example: sun ___S___   nose ___Z___

1. fuss _____   4. save _____

2. fuse _____   5. wise _____

3. us _____   6. kiss _____

D.

One word in each row is a SIGHT WORD. Circle it. *(2 points)*

1.   yes   yet   yell   you
2.   cope   cone   come   cove

E.

Fill in the blanks to complete the rule about the sound of the letter **g**.
(3 points)

> The letter **g** will sound like / j / if the
>
> letter ____ , ____ , or ____ comes after the **g**.

F.

Write **G** if the **g** letter sounds like / g /. Write **J** if the **g** letter sounds like
/ j /. *(6 points)*

Example: gem ___J___   gum ___G___

   1. got _____   **4.** hug _____

   2. gym _____   **5.** huge _____

   3. age _____   **6.** gate _____

G.

Write CONSONANT if the **y** letter is a consonant. Write VOWEL if the **y**
letter is a VOWEL. *(6 points)*

Example: yell _consonant_   lady _vowel_

   1. yet _____

   2. type _____

   3. happy _____

   4. you _____

   5. gym _____

   6. my _____

H.

Fill in the blanks to make each sentence complete. Use the words from the list below. *(5 points)*

box	fix	tax	quit	quite

1. Sue _____ her job at the mill.

2. Did you _____ the hole in the fence yet?

3. Max will buy a _____ of candy for his girl.

4. The bus ride made the man _____ ill.

5. Will the _____ rate go up in June?

I.

Write the KEY WORDS for the short vowel sounds that the teacher will say. *(5 points)*

1. _____   4. _____

2. _____   5. _____

3. _____

J.

Listen, then circle the word that the teacher says. *(8 points)*

1.	rig	rag	rage	rug
2.	fun	fan	fin	fine
3.	robe	rob	rub	rib
4.	cap	cop	cup	cope
5.	quote	quake	quite	quit
6.	came	cam	can	cane
7.	got	gut	gate	get
8.	cube	cub	cut	cute

Read the directions with the teacher.

A.

Match each word in Column A with its definition in Column B. Write the letter of your answer on the line next to the number. *(8 points)*

	Column A	**Column B**
_____	**1.** damp	**a.** cut
_____	**2.** swift	**b.** not tame
_____	**3.** snip	**c.** fast
_____	**4.** grin	**d.** wet
_____	**5.** dwell	**e.** stop
_____	**6.** blaze	**c.** live
_____	**7.** wild	**d.** smile
_____	**8.** halt	**e.** fire

B.

One word in each row is a SIGHT WORD. Circle it. *(2 points)*

1. size   sign   side   site
2. twist   twice   twin   two

C.

Draw a line from each word in the left column to a word that means the OPPOSITE in the right column. *(5 points)*

small   run
hard   true
sharp   large
off   soft
walk   dull
false   on

D.

Fill in each blank with the correct word. *(8 points)*

1. A glass lamp fell from the _____ and broke.

disk   desk

2. The baby in the sandpile had a _____ on his face.

grim   grin

3. Next time, I can cut the grass _____ .

yourself   myself

4. The guard had a large red _____ on his arm.

scarf   scar

5. Is the water in the tub still _____ ?

warn   warm

6. A cop drove to the crime lab in a _____ car.

squad   squat

7. The small child held a bug in the _____ of her hand.

palm   part

8. Mark _____ to get some gas for the car.

want   went

E.

Divide these compound words. *(5 points)*

1. himself   = _____ + _____

2. sidewalk = _____ + _____

3. classmate = _____ + _____

4. wildlife   = _____ + _____

5. lifeguard = _____ + _____

F.

Follow the directions. *(11 points)*

1. Write the word **slim**. _____

2. Change the *m* to *p*. _____

3. Change the *i* to *a*. _____

4. Change the *s* to *f*. _____

5. Change the *a* to *o*. _____

6. Change the *o* to *i*. _____

7. Change the *f* to *c*. _____

8. Change the *i* to *a*. _____

9. Change the *p* to *m*. _____

10. Change the *c* to *s*. _____

11. Change the *a* to *i*. _____

G.

The teacher will pronounce six words. Write the LETTER of the short vowel that you hear in each word. *(6 points)*

1. _____   3. _____   5. _____

2. _____   4. _____   6. _____

H.

Listen, then circle the word the teacher says. *(6 points)*

1.	sign	sin	sun	sane
2.	mast	most	must	mist
3.	stall	stale	style	still
4.	band	bond	bend	bind
5.	bake	bark	brake	broke

Read the directions with the teacher.

<u>A.</u>

Join each root word and its affix. *(5 points)*

1. use   +   ing   =   _____

2. haze   +   y   =   _____

3. file   +   ed   =   _____

4. fill   +   ed   =   _____

5. ice   +   y   =   _____

<u>B.</u>

Fill in each blank with the correct word. *(5 points)*

1. The root word of **hoping** is _____ .

2. The root word of **fussy** is _____ .

3. The root word of **named** is _____ .

4. The root word of **dining** is _____ .

5. The root word of **baby** is _____ .

<u>C.</u>

Separate each root word from its affix. *(5 points)*

1. _____   +   _____   =   baking

2. _____   +   _____   =   nosy

3. _____   +   _____   =   crossed

4. _____   +   _____   =   typing

5. _____   +   _____   =   cured

Student Book 1
Part 4 *cont.*
(50 points)

D.

Draw a line from each word in the left column to a word that means the OPPOSITE in the right column. *(5 points)*

hated	taking
going	fired
started	loved
giving	coming
hired	ended

E.

One word in each row is a sight word. Circle it. *(2 points)*

1. send   sand   said   side
2. are   arm   art   ark

F.

Follow the directions. *(6 points)*

1. Write the word **rent.** _____
2. Change the *e* to *a*. _____
3. Take away the *n*. _____
4. Change the *a* to *u*. _____
5. Add *n* after the *u*. _____
6. Change the *u* to *e*. _____

G.

Fill in the blank to complete the Silent **e** Spelling Rule. *(1 point)*

> If a word ends with a silent **e**, drop the **e** before
> adding an affix that starts with a _____ .

H.

Put these words in ALPHABETICAL ORDER. *(10 points)*

1. job _____ **2.** quit _____

     haze _____   scar _____

     file _____   old _____

     fill _____   smart _____

     ice _____   plan _____

I.

Fill in each blank with a word from the word list. *(7 points)*

1. The sun is _____ .

2. Will the plane be _____ at 7:30?

3. My boss is _____ more men for the job.

4. His old car was _____ him a lot of money.

5. I am _____ a postcard to my father.

6. We were _____ the large box into the cart.

7. Fog was _____ in from the lake.

WORD LIST
costing
drifting
hiring
landing
lifting
rising
sending

J.

Listen, then circle the word that the teacher says. *(4 points)*

1. side said sad sod

2. faced fast fussed fist

3. boss bass base bus

4. mile mill mall male